WILLIAM GAMINARA

William Gaminara's adaptation of Zola's *Germinal* was toured by Paines Plough Theatre Company in 1988. His screenplay *Infantile Disorders* (made by the Children's Film Unit) was shown on Channel 4 in 1989. His first original stage-play *Back Up the Hearse and Let Them Sniff the Flowers* was presented at Hampstead Theatre, London in April 1993, following which he received a commission to write *According to Hoyle*.

William Gaminara

ACCORDING
TO HOYLE

NICK HERN BOOKS
London
www.nickhernbooks.co.uk

A Nick Hern Book

According to Hoyle first published in Great Britain in 1996 as a paperback original by Nick Hern Books, 14 Larden Road, London W3 7ST

Reprinted 2006, 2010

According to Hoyle copyright © 1996 by William Gaminara

Typeset by Country Setting, Kingsdown, Kent CT14 8ES
Printed in Great Britain by CLE Print Ltd, St Ives, Cambs, PE27 3LE

A CIP catalogue record for this book is available from the British Library

ISBN   978 1 85459 355 9

According to Hoyle was first performed at the Hampstead
Theatre, London, on 7 December 1995, with the following
cast:

MICKY   Robert Glenister
CLIVE   Jonathan Coy
KEVIN   Trevor Cooper
CHRIS   Nick Dunning
EDDIE   Peter Hugo-Daly

Director   Robin Lefèvre
Designer   Sue Plummer
Lighting Designer   Gerry Jenkinson
Sound Designer   Simon Whitehorn

ACCORDING TO HOYLE

Characters

All in their late thirties or thereabouts

MICKY

CLIVE

KEVIN

CHRIS

EDDIE

**All dialogue relating exclusively to the cards/betting
is in bold print, thus**

The Set

The scenes of the play alternate between a single evening in the
present and several different evenings during the past two years.
On many occasions it will be possible simply to dim the lights to
indicate a time change. Sometimes however it will be necessary
for a blackout as characters will need to enter or exit from the
stage unseen. Apart from the interval there are no physical scene
changes at all.

ACT ONE

CHRIS*'s flat. The Present. We are in a large kitchen. There are a number of cardboard boxes lying around, some of which are empty, a few of which have been packed. There is a door leading to the garden and a door leading to the rest of the house, out of which* CHRIS *and* EDDIE *are trying to manoeuvre a large kitchen table.*

CHRIS. Pull it!

EDDIE. I am pulling it! It's not going to go.

CHRIS. Push it then. (*Beat.*) Harder.

EDDIE. Mind my fingers.

CHRIS. To the left.

EDDIE. I am. Jesus.

CHRIS. Go on! To the LEFT!

EDDIE. WHOSE LEFT?

CHRIS. Mine of course.

EDDIE. Thank you. Now I know. Mind my fingers.

CHRIS. Easy . . .

EDDIE. It won't go.

CHRIS. Yes it will. Lift it higher.

EDDIE. It won't go!

CHRIS. It will if you lift it higher.

They heave it up higher.

EDDIE. Shit!

CHRIS. What's the matter?

EDDIE. Put it down.

CHRIS. What's the . . .

EDDIE. Just put it down.

They put the table down. EDDIE *nurses his hand in agonised silence.*

I told you.

CHRIS. What is it?

EDDIE. My finger.

CHRIS. Sorry.

Pause.

Is it an important one?

EDDIE. Yes. I've got a gig tonight. And a date.

Pause.

It's not going to go. Not unless you chop its bloody legs off.

CHRIS *examines the table legs.*

I wasn't being serious.

CHRIS. Why not?

EDDIE. What are we going to play on?

CHRIS. I wouldn't do it now.

EDDIE. It's a bit drastic isn't it? This table's been with us since the start. It's got a collective memory of every game that's been lost and won.

CHRIS. That's why I want to get rid of it.

EDDIE. If we were Red Indians we'd be polishing it. WORSHIPPING it . . . not talking about cutting its legs off.

CHRIS. You suggested it! Anyway, God knows where I've packed the saw. We might as well leave it here. It is the last game. Give us a hand will you.

EDDIE. The last game? The last game HERE.

They move the table back into the room.

Though I'm beginning to wonder. Standards are definitely slipping. Last time we played, Kevin was looking at his watch by eleven-thirty. Eleven-thirty! I thought for a minute he was going to ask for a cup of Ovaltine. And then I got shouted at by you for blowing smoke over the table. If you'd said that ten years ago you'd have been lynched. Seven o'clock start, break at midnight for narcotics, last deal as the sun came up. Now it's all herbal cigarettes and guava juice. Since when did people play Poker to keep fit?

CHRIS *opens a cupboard and takes out a quarterful bottle of whisky. He looks for a suitable place to hide it, deciding in the end to put it in one of the cardboard boxes. He continues packing.* EDDIE *rolls himself a cigarette.*

See what I mean?

CHRIS. Are you going to help or are you just going to stand around?

EDDIE. Stand around. It's safer.

Pause.

Are you out of here next week?

CHRIS. Monday.

EDDIE. Monday! (*Pause.*) You're cutting it fine. When's the big day?

CHRIS. Three weeks tomorrow.

EDDIE. Are you nervous?

CHRIS. No I'm looking forward to it.

EDDIE. Really? (*Pause.*) Who's the Best Man?

CHRIS. We're not having one. There's a Best Woman.

EDDIE. Oh right.

CHRIS. One of Clare's friends.

EDDIE. Don't get me wrong, but doesn't it worry you to think that from now on Clare might be the only woman you ever sleep with. Ever again. In your whole life?

CHRIS. So?

EDDIE. I just wondered.

CHRIS. That's the whole idea actually. (*Beat.*) Come on, give us a hand.

EDDIE. I've got to get to the bookies before five-thirty.

CHRIS. Plenty of time.

EDDIE *holds his stomach.*

What's wrong?

EDDIE. Guts. Last night's curry.

He watches CHRIS *packing.*

Clive's definitely coming, is he?

CHRIS. Yes.

EDDIE. How is he?

CHRIS. He said he'd had a bit of a 'domestic hiccough'.

EDDIE. Oh? (*Beat.*) What?

CHRIS. He didn't say. Seriously Eddie I do need a hand.

EDDIE. Alright, alright. What's the plan . . . shift the stuff out the front and then play? Or play and then shift . . . shift a little, play a little and then shift a little more?

EDDIE exits carrying a box. CHRIS opens a cupboard and stares into it. EDDIE enters quietly behind him.

Chris?

CHRIS. What?

EDDIE. What is it?

CHRIS. Just something of Micky's I'd missed. A mug I gave him for his birthday. I keep doing this. Stumbling on little bits of him in unexpected corners. I ran into his sister last week. Do you know for about a minute I couldn't remember her name. I've known her for nearly thirty years and I could not remember her name.

EDDIE. It happens.

CHRIS. I'd also promised I'd keep in touch but I haven't.

EDDIE. Why not?

CHRIS. I don't know.

EDDIE. Yeah well . . . that's what comes of being a feckless bastard.

He lifts up a cardboard box and heads for the door.

CHRIS. What?

EDDIE. That's what comes of being a feckless bastard.

He exits. CHRIS freezes for a moment as if caught in a memory. As he closes the cupboard door, the lights snap to a different state. It is nearly two years earlier.

CLIVE and CHRIS prepare the table. MICKY enters.

MICKY. Can I just say that if we really are going ahead with this . . .

CLIVE. How long have we got?

CHRIS. Oh . . . half an hour.

MICKY. I didn't realise . . . I thought it was a joke. So we are, are we?

CLIVE. Of course we are.

MICKY. Fine. Well in that case I am seriously going to need some more clothes.

CHRIS. What for?

MICKY. Well look at me! I'm really not wearing very much. And it's the one day I've come out without a vest on. For some reason when I got up this morning I didn't put it on. Why not? Why today of all days, did I decide not to?

CLIVE. It was obviously meant to be.

MICKY. Meant to be what?

CHRIS. You'll be fine. Sort out the chairs, will you.

MICKY. I don't want to be fine, I want to be dressed.

Picks up a chair.

CHRIS. Where's Kevin?

CLIVE. He's coming. I assume we're going to fix the pack.

MICKY. Are we? It's not exactly cricket.

CLIVE. We're not exactly playing cricket. (*Taking the chairs.*) Shall I relieve you of those, Micky, we don't want you to rupture your ovaries.

MICKY. Which of you actually spoke to them anyway?

CLIVE. We both did.

MICKY. And what did they say? Exactly. I mean . . . it's definitely going to happen?

CLIVE. Yes.

MICKY. Great.

Pause. CHRIS *produces the baize and spreads it out over the table.* CLIVE *arranges the chairs.*

We're a bit old for this really, aren't we? I thought this kind of thing was supposed to happen when you were about fifteen.

Pause.

They definitely know that we're playing STRIP-poker?

CLIVE. Of course they know.

MICKY. And they were agreeable?

CLIVE. Very!

CHRIS. In fact they suggested it. Didn't they?

CLIVE. Er . . .

MICKY. THEY did?

CLIVE. Yes I think maybe they did.

MICKY. Look, I don't want to go on about this . . .

CLIVE. You are.

MICKY. . . . but if they're not on for it, I for one don't think we should be doing this. If there's any question of false pretences . . . then the whole thing gets rather tasteless and I'd really rather not have anything to do with it . . . (*Beat.*) Chris?

CHRIS. Well . . .

CLIVE. I think it's horribly chauvinistic of you to assume that women are incapable of, or unwilling to, initiate sexual activity. If they decide they want to participate in leisure activities that involve the partial or total removal of their clothing for whatever reason, I really don't think it's up to you or I as men to suggest that that is wrong. They are after all masters of . . .

CHRIS. Mistresses . . .

CLIVE. Mistresses . . . of their own bodies. It is ultimately a question of freedom of choice, irrespective of gender.

MICKY (*beat*). Yes. Yes I suppose so.

CLIVE. Right then. Where are the chips?

CHRIS. Third drawer down.

CLIVE. Cards?

CHRIS. In the front-room. On the mantelpiece.

MICKY. I'm just going upstairs for a second.

MICKY *exits.*

CLIVE. Hook line and sinker.

CHRIS. That was awesome.

KEVIN (*off*). Mind your back.

MICKY (*off*). Sorry.

CHRIS. Positively awesome.

CLIVE. It was rather impressive, wasn't it. Almost faultless. It just seemed to burble up from nowhere.

KEVIN *enters carrying a box.*

KEVIN. The milky bars are on me!

He puts the box down on the table and takes the things out one by one.

Six packets of crisps, two salt and vinegar, two roast chicken and two prawn, three twiglets, two cheese puffs, eight bags of hoolahoops, one Toblerone and a king size fruit and nut. And that's just the hors d'oeuvre. (*Tommy Cooper laugh.*)

CHRIS. I was really hoping for something a little less nutritious.

KEVIN (*holding up the hoola hoops*). I did a commercial for these once. I had to eat forty-three bags in four hours. Forty-three. And then I had to eat the hoolahops. (*Tommy Cooper laugh. He hands* CHRIS *his keys.*) What's up with Micky? He's looking green.

CLIVE. Excitement.

KEVIN. How's his father?

CHRIS. They're moving him to hospital.

KEVIN. Sounds serious.

CHRIS. It is. Micky's delighted.

CLIVE. We've managed to convince him . . .

CHRIS. WE haven't . . . YOU have.

CLIVE. I'VE managed to convince him that a couple of girls Chris was . . .

CHRIS. Women.

CLIVE. I've managed to convince him that a couple of wimmin Chris was chatting up earlier on in the pub . . .

CHRIS. To.

CLIVE. Will you stop interrupting.

CHRIS. To!

CLIVE. What?

CHRIS. Chatting TO . . . not UP.

CLIVE. Whatever . . . I've convinced him that they're coming over to play strip-poker.

KEVIN. What!

CHRIS. Which they're not.

KEVIN. Oh right. Pity. Can't think why not.

CLIVE. Not even Chris could pull that off. Not for want of trying, though. When he casually mentioned that not only did he enjoy ironing but that he'd once shared a taxi with Germaine Greer, one of them positively wet herself. Whether it was from excitement or from sheer disbelief at the idea that this was in any way impressive, we shall never know.

CHRIS. Actually we might. (*Beat.*) One of them IS coming over.

CLIVE *is unconvinced.*

To play. Ordinary poker.

Pause.

Is there a problem?

CLIVE. You are joking, I hope.

KEVIN. Why not?

CLIVE. You have unilaterally invited someone to join the game without any consultation whatsoever?

CHRIS. Yes. Fresh blood . . . what's wrong with that?

CLIVE. A woman.

CHRIS. Yes.

CLIVE. Next month we will be celebrating the eighteenth anniversary of this Poker school. Not once in that time have we ever played with a woman.

CHRIS. Well it's about time then.

CLIVE. Don't pretend that it won't make any difference to the game.

KEVIN. It makes a difference whoever joins.

CLIVE. Not the same difference. Which one?

CHRIS (*to* KEVIN). Alright with you?

KEVIN. Sure. What's she like?

CHRIS. She's nice.

KEVIN. She can't be that nice if she wants to play poker with us. (*Tommy Cooper laugh.*) Seriously, what's she like?

CHRIS. I said . . . she's nice!

KEVIN. Yes but . . . you know . . .

CHRIS. What?

CLIVE. Oh just tell him whether she's the good-looking one or not for God's sake . . .

CHRIS. I'm not going to pander to your smutty little . . .

CLIVE. There's nothing smutty about it. Either she is or she isn't. Or were you too busy admiring her intellect and personality to notice?

CHRIS. I'm not going to anwer.

CLIVE (*to* KEVIN). It's the ugly one.

CHRIS. Clive!

CLIVE (*getting up*). Ugly as sin.

CLIVE *exits.*

CHRIS. Hook, line and sinker.

KEVIN. What?

CHRIS. I'm just giving Clive a taste of his own medicine. For being so offensive.

KEVIN. She's not coming either?

CHRIS. No.

KEVIN. Oh. Am I here, or am I a figment of someone's imagination as well?

CHRIS. I DID ask her. Both of them.

KEVIN. What did they say?

CHRIS. They said they'd think about it. But they won't. I wouldn't. (*Hands him the chips.*) Count those out, will you.

Pause.

How's work?

KEVIN. I'm doing another 'Bill' next week. Otherwise nothing. I haven't done a radio play for six months. I used to do one a week. I don't know what's happening. I think I'm just going to have to do my own thing. A bit of stand-up or something. Take control. I could do with a few laughs. Four Bills in three years! It's like a jail sentence.

CHRIS. Are you playing a . . .

KEVIN. Yes. An Inspector.

CHRIS. Promotion. You must be doing something right.

KEVIN. Yeah. Growing older. (*Tommy Cooper laugh.*)

CLIVE *enters carrying the cards.*

CLIVE. I think you should also know that it being the last Friday of the month I have no intention whatsoever of modifying my behaviour. I intend to fart, belch and swear as much as I am humanly able.

KEVIN. Lucky us.

CHRIS. There are pills you can take to lower your testosterone levels you know.

CLIVE. They also make you grow breasts.

KEVIN. Ooh!

CHRIS. I think it's about time you surrendered a little part of your masculinity for the sake of the common good.

CLIVE. Surely even you would draw the line at growing breasts. In any case, speaking as the only man here to have been married once let alone three times, it will not have escaped your notice that I've spent most of the last twenty years surrendering parts of my masculinity. In fact I'm rapidly running out of parts TO surrender.

He sits down with the cards.

CHRIS. What's Micky up to?

CLIVE. I've no idea.

KEVIN. Tell me . . .

CHRIS. What?

KEVIN. You've known him longest . . . do you think he's still a virgin?

CHRIS. God knows.

KEVIN. Tilly says he is.

CHRIS. How would she know?

KEVIN. She reckons she can tell just by looking. Mind you she is blind as a bat. She'd have to be to end up with a fat git like me. (*Tommy Cooper laugh.*) No, it's just that I can't IMAGINE anyone Micky's age being a virgin . . . and yet I can't imagine him NOT being one somehow. I could understand someone wanting to mug him or talk him down from a window-sill . . . but I couldn't understand anyone wanting to stick their tongue in his ear.

CLIVE (*getting up*). The English are not very discriminating about who they go to bed with.

He opens the back door and stands in the doorway facing the garden.

CHRIS (*to* CLIVE). What are you doing?

CLIVE. What does it look like?

KEVIN. An-i-mal.

CHRIS. Could you not go just a little further into the garden?

CLIVE. I'm sorry but I tend to leave these things to the last minute . . . always have done apparently, it used to drive my mother mad.

KEVIN. You should be grateful it's not the sink again.

CLIVE. Relax. Without wishing to brag I can actually clear this flowerpot and reach the flowerbed from here.

MICKY enters. He is wearing two shirts, a tie and a kind of après-ski anorak, all belonging to CHRIS.

MICKY. Do rings count?

They all turn and stare at him.

CLIVE. I'm not sure you're entering into the spirit of the game.

CHRIS. You look like me.

MICKY. Do I? You don't mind do you?

KEVIN. You look very sexy. Have a crisp?

MICKY. No thanks.

KEVIN. 'One minute from now you'll wish you'd had one.'

MICKY. It occurred to me . . . a technicality I suppose . . . but even so . . . what happens if one of us . . . WHEN one of us . . . or one of them rather . . . preferably . . . (*To* CHRIS.) . . . what are their names by the way?

CLIVE *and* CHRIS. Rebecca.

MICKY (*Beat.*) What, they're both called Rebecca?

CHRIS. I can't remember.

MICKY. Well what happens when Rebecca or . . . whatever her name is . . . and I think as a common courtesy we should find out . . . what happens when she or we haven't got any clothes on?

CHRIS. I've no idea. Ask Clive.

CLIVE. Oh dear.

CHRIS. What?

CLIVE. There's a pair of boots in the flower-pot. Apologies.

CHRIS. Oh God.

CLIVE. Rather a foolish place to leave them it must be said. Is there a tap out here?

CHRIS. Round to the right.

CLIVE (*finishing*). Your new neighbours seem very friendly.

He disappears further into the garden.

MICKY. So here we go then. Countdown.

Pause.

KEVIN. How's the novel going Micky?

MICKY. Alright thanks. You know. Three steps forward, two steps back. It's a race against time really.

KEVIN. Have you got a deadline?

MICKY. Not as such. But it would be nice to finish it before I die.

CHRIS. I've been having a go at something as a matter of fact.

MICKY. Have you?

CHRIS. Just for fun. A couple of stories.

MICKY. Great. How's it going?

CHRIS. Fine. I've nearly finished.

MICKY. Have you? (*Beat.*) It's different with a novel of course. And I do like to plan a lot. Probably too much. I think that's why I had to start again. Again. (*Beat.*) What are you going to do with them?

CHRIS. God knows. Burn them I expect.

MICKY. That's the hard part. Getting anyone interested. Well if you want me to have a look at them some time . . .

CHRIS. I would, thanks.

Pause.

MICKY (*to* KEVIN). Does my breath smell?

He breathes on him.

KEVIN. No, it doesn't smell in the . . .

He does a mock faint.

MICKY. No seriously.

KEVIN. Sweet as roses.

Pause.

MICKY. My hands have gone all sweaty, has anyone else . . .

CHRIS. They're not coming.

MICKY. Who's not coming?

CHRIS. The women.

MICKY. They've cancelled?

CHRIS. They were never coming.

MICKY. They lied? (*Pause.*) Oh I see.

CHRIS. Sorry.

MICKY. I knew it. Whose idea was that?

KEVIN. Who do you think?

MICKY (*laughs with relief*). Shit. I was really looking forward to it.

CLIVE *enters.*

CLIVE. I can't find it. It's pitch black out there. But I'm told urine's very good for leather.

CHRIS. I'll do it. I've only had those boots a month.

CHRIS *exits into the garden.*

CLIVE. Greater love hath no man. Everyone alright?

MICKY. Fine.

KEVIN. Fine.

MICKY. I'll think I'll go and slip into something cooler if you don't mind.

CLIVE. It is a little excessive. It'll take the best part of a week just to get you down to your underwear. (*Looks at his watch.*) They shouldn't be too long now.

MICKY. I can't wait.

MICKY *exits. Pause. We hear the sound of water splashing outside.*

CLIVE. I feel rather insulted.

KEVIN. Why?

CLIVE. Do you think Chris really expects me to believe all that crap about a woman coming along? His ability to lie convincingly is clearly dwindling. He needs a relationship badly.

KEVIN. I don't think it is crap.

CLIVE. Oh?

KEVIN. No, no. Apparently they were just having a drink and . . . he and this woman . . . and somehow the conversation . . . I can't remember how exactly but the conversation got onto cards and . . . he asked her if she'd like to come and play cards . . . poker . . . and she said . . . yes.

CLIVE. Bluffing never was your strongest department was it Kevin.

KEVIN. It's true!

CHRIS *enters from the garden.*

CHRIS. Thirty-eight and you're still not toilet trained. (*To* KEVIN.) Everything alright?

KEVIN. Fine. I think.

CHRIS. At what point exactly were you proposing to put Micky out of his misery?

CLIVE. At what point exactly were you proposing to put me out of my misery?

CHRIS. How do you mean?

CLIVE. Kevin has just unwittingly confirmed what I already knew, namely that charming as you are, master of concealment as you are or at least were, you don't really think I believe . . .

The doorbell rings. They freeze.

Ye Gods!

MICKY *bursts in half-undressed.*

MICKY. I thought you said they weren't coming . . .

CHRIS. They weren't!

Snap blackout. When the lights come up again they are in their previous state. The Present. CHRIS stands facing EDDIE.

EDDIE. Who?

CHRIS. Who what?

EDDIE. You just said . . . 'I wish it HAD been them instead of you.'

Pause.

CHRIS. Did I? (*Pause.*) Success?

EDDIE. Sexy Sadie, fourteen to one, Catford.

CHRIS. Fourteen to one! How much did you win?

EDDIE. She hasn't run yet. I just put the bet on. It's downhill from now on. But I once had a girlfriend called Sadie so I couldn't not.

CHRIS. Is that how you pick all your bets?

EDDIE. Sometimes. It cuts down the choice.

CHRIS. Not by much.

EDDIE. It's intuitive really. I picked Shergar long before anyone had even heard of him.

CHRIS. You had a girlfriend called Shergar?

EDDIE. No. Instinct. I'm talking about following your instincts.

EDDIE *sees a packet of new plastic chips lying on the sideboard.*

What the hell are these?

CHRIS. I thought the old ones were looking a bit . . . old.

EDDIE. These are horrible. They're all new.

CHRIS. You're the one who's always going on about changing the stakes.

EDDIE. The stakes, not the chips. I can't play with these. Let's stick with the others.

CHRIS. Suit yourself. That's ready to go if you're . . .

EDDIE. Listen, don't ask me to lift anything else, I can't risk it, not with this. (*He shows his finger.*)

CHRIS. Django Reinhardt only had two fingers.

EDDIE. Much easier with only two. The others don't keep getting in the way.

CHRIS *continues packing.*

Where is everyone? I'm the only one who has to come on public transport and I'm the first to arrive.

CHRIS. They'll come.

EDDIE. I thought you said six o'clock.

CHRIS. I did. You were an hour early.

EDDIE. Was I? (*Pause.* EDDIE *holds up a pack.*) Cut for a fiver?

CHRIS. Alright. Shuffle first.

EDDIE *shuffles.*

EDDIE. It must be strange moving out of here. It seems like only yesterday you arrived.

CHRIS. Not to me. More like a lifetime.

A look is exchanged.

EDDIE. Is that why Clare's never moved in?

CHRIS. Jesus Eddie, what do you think?

EDDIE. I don't know. I don't have to live here.

CHRIS. Why do you think I'm moving? I couldn't set foot in the bathroom for six weeks. It's been six months now and it's still like stepping into somebody else's grave. I get in and I get out as fast as I can. And it's like that all over. Every room's got a different memory, clawing at you. Drop your guard for a second and they drag you under.

Pause.

I think they're probably shuffled by now.

EDDIE. Sorry. They never found out where Micky went, did they. After he left here?

CHRIS. No.

EDDIE. I've never said this to you before because I didn't think it was necessary but . . . it wasn't your fault you know.

CHRIS. Did I say it was?

EDDIE. No. But sometimes you talk as if it was.

Pause.

How much?

CHRIS. **Five**

EDDIE. **Done.**

EDDIE *cuts the pack and holds up his card.* CHRIS *continues packing throughout this sequence.*

Eight of clubs.

He offers the pack to CHRIS. *He cuts.*

CHRIS. **Ten. Bad luck.**

EDDIE. **Double or quits?**

CHRIS. **Okay.**

EDDIE *cuts again.*

EDDIE. **Three of bloody diamonds.**

He holds the pack for CHRIS *who cuts.*

CHRIS. **Nine.**

EDDIE. It's going to be that kind of an evening is it. **Double or quits.**

He cuts again.

Queen. That's more like it.

CHRIS. Cut for me will you?

EDDIE. What?

CHRIS. Cut for me. I need to keep going.

EDDIE *cuts again.*

EDDIE. Oh for fuck's sake!

CHRIS. What is it?

EDDIE. **A king.** It's bad enough being beaten by you, now I'm beating myself. **Double or quits.**

CHRIS. No.

EDDIE (*beat.*) What do you mean 'no'?

CHRIS. No.

EDDIE. You've got to.

CHRIS. No I don't. You owe me twenty quid.

The doorbell rings.

Clive.

EDDIE. Bastard. Double or quits says it's Kevin.

CHRIS. Done.

CHRIS *presses the automatic entry. They stare at the door.* CLIVE *enters.*

Hi Clive. (*To* EDDIE.) Forty.

EDDIE. How could you tell?

CLIVE. Greetings, gentlemen.

CHRIS. Kevin said he'd be late. Don't worry, you know what they say . . . unlucky at cards . . .

CLIVE. My God it looks grim in here. I always said it was a dump. Isn't time you elbowed this Legal Aid malarkey and made some dosh?

EDDIE. You're late.

CLIVE. Losing already, Eddie?

EDDIE. No. Well . . . yes.

CLIVE *goes to the cupboard from which* CHRIS *took the whisky bottle. Unable to find it, he searches casually through all the other cupboards, drawers, shelves etc.* CHRIS *watches.*

We said six o'clock.

CHRIS. It doesn't matter.

CLIVE. You know you'll never be a rock-star Eddie if you fret quite so obsessively over punctuality. I thought that was about the first thing they taught you at the Keith Moon Academy.

CHRIS. How are the kids? Is Misha alright?

CLIVE. As alright as she ever will be.

CHRIS. Steven?

CLIVE. Apart from the fact that he's got me for a father and Sally for a mother, yes. Why?

CHRIS. You mentioned there was a problem.

CLIVE. Nothing that a bullet in the back of the head can't solve. In the meantime in the absence of any bullets . . . (*Finding the whisky.*) Ah!

EDDIE. Whose head?

CHRIS. How did you know it was there?

CLIVE. Sixth sense. What's it doing there anyway?

CHRIS. It must have been put there by mistake.

CLIVE (*pouring himself a whisky*). So. The final game.

EDDIE. Here.

CLIVE. But of course. Where's Kevin?

CHRIS. He's coming late and going early.

CLIVE. Why?

CHRIS. I don't know. I spoke to Tilly.

CLIVE. Cheers.

They watch him down a substantial whisky.

Better already. No, my offspring are in fine form. Misha mercifully spends her whole time avoiding me so she clearly has some moderately unsavoury boyfriend in tow at the moment which is reassuring because if he was REALLY unsavoury she'd have made a point of parading him in front of me. Steven, having decided at last that nappies are not where it's at, has subsequently defecated in every room in the house.

CHRIS. Chip off the old block.

CLIVE. Thank God he's only there weekends.

He drinks.

So what about you, Eddie. What have you been up to?

EDDIE. Me? This and that.

CLIVE. Fascinating. We don't appear to have a quorum yet. Does that mean we have to lug boxes around or are we allowed a gentle three-hander?

EDDIE. I'm not lugging any boxes around.

CHRIS. He's got a runny tummy and a sore finger.

CLIVE. Poor lamb. (*Passes the bottle.*) Try some of this.

CHRIS (*to* EDDIE). Your cards.

EDDIE *shuffles.*

CLIVE. How's Clare?

CHRIS. She's well. She's very excited. So am I.

CLIVE. I can't imagine why. You must be mad. You look terrible.

CHRIS. I've had a funeral, a wedding and moved house all within six months.

CLIVE. Just the divorce to go then.

CHRIS. I think I'm entitled to look terrible.

EDDIE (*as he deals*). And suddenly the temperature soars to a hundred and ten degrees, there's not a drop of water to be found and your only companion is a prickly pear, all of which means it's time for a game of . . . Mexican Sweat. **Clive to turn.**

They each have seven cards in front of them faced downwards.

CLIVE (*turns a card*). **The ten of clubs. Modest yet assertive. All the way.** (*They bet.*) Yes, it's been an interesting week. There I was at the traffic-lights the other morning on my way to the gallery . . .

CHRIS (*turning cards*). **A pair of sixes. All the way.**

CLIVE. When three squeegies or whatever they like to call themselves pounced on me . . .

EDDIE *turns his cards.*

One on each side and one rather large one in front just to make sure I couldn't make a quick getaway.

EDDIE. **And it's a pair of nines. No bet.**

CLIVE. **All the way.** A bit keen for eight-thirty in the morning. I thought they were going to give me an M.O.T. Anyway . . . (*He turns his cards.*) . . . having made it perfectly clear via various unambiguous hand signals that I didn't want the car touched let alone washed . . . **pair of kings . . . all the way . . .** and that I certainly wasn't going to give any money to them for something I didn't want doing in the first place, all three of them came and stood in front of me. Or rather slouched in front of me.

CHRIS *turns his cards.*

And then the lights changed.

EDDIE. So what happened?

CLIVE. I revved the engine as a declaration of intent. Which was duly ignored.

CHRIS. **Yes! Two pairs, aces and sixes.**

CLIVE. And then I drove off.

CHRIS. You didn't give them anything?

CLIVE. Apart from several broken bones, not a penny, no.

CHRIS. **All the way**.

CLIVE. But as I drove off, I looked back to inspect the damage.

CHRIS. Your cards, Eddie.

CLIVE. And guess who I saw?

EDDIE (*beat.*) Who?

CLIVE. Sally.

CHRIS. What was she doing?

CLIVE. Getting on a bus.

CHRIS. So?

CLIVE. Well, apart from the fact that Sally never slums it on buses. And it was eight-thirty in the morning. And she was nowhere near where she's allegedly been staying. Nothing.

　　EDDIE turns his last card.

CHRIS. Was she alone?

CLIVE. I don't know.

EDDIE. **Fold.** Maybe she's just been staying somewhere else and she hasn't told you yet.

CLIVE. Evidently.

　　He turns his card and stares at it.

EDDIE. **Three kings**. You've won.

CLIVE. I don't really give a flying fuck to be honest. But it does rather give the lie to all the bull-shit I've been getting about wanting to get back together again. Still, good luck to her.

EDDIE. Aren't you rather jumping to conclusions?

CHRIS. Yes.

EDDIE. I mean two and two don't always make four.

CLIVE. I beg your pardon?

EDDIE (*beat*). Well obviously they DO but . . .

CLIVE. Is this the basis of your poker strategy, because if it is it explains an awful lot.

EDDIE. What I mean is . . . she could have been doing anything.

CLIVE. Such as?

EDDIE. She could have been . . . she could have been . . .

CHRIS. Shopping.

EDDIE. Shopping.

CLIVE. Shopping.

EDDIE. Yes. Or just . . . just going somewhere.

CLIVE. Well I'm almost as impressed by your inventiveness as I am touched by your faith in human nature. However, as far as Sally's concerned I'm afraid you've rather missed the mark, she has single-handedly redefined the limits of deviousness . . .

CHRIS. Oh come on.

CLIVE. . . . and is clearly having an affair. (*Pause.*) I've won, have I?

EDDIE. Yes.

Pause.

CLIVE (*collecting the pot*). Presumably he, she or it was on the bus with her. The driver I expect, anything for a free ride. I don't really care very much. Which isn't to say I couldn't happily strangle them both. I suppose it makes me an eligible bachelor again in a funny kind of way. Fourth time lucky. (*Picking up the bottle of whisky.*) Is this really the sum total of all the whisky in this house?

CHRIS. I'm afraid it is.

CLIVE. Well that's not going to last the evening is it.

EDDIE *suddenly jumps up and runs out of the room clutching his stomach.*

What's the matter with him?

CHRIS (*following him*). Eddie . . . the bathroom Eddie . . . the bathroom!

He exits. CLIVE *sits on his own for a second. The lights fade as he pours the last drops of whisky into his glass.*

When they go up again the room is empty. It is one month on from the previous past scene. CHRIS *enters at speed, goes over to the answering machine and switches it on. He moves to the table and starts sorting out chips, cards and chairs. Over this and the following action the messages play back.*

Answering-machine. First message:

MICKY. 'Chris . . . hi, it's me. Micky. I hope you're well. I was really wondering about Friday. I'm assuming it's all on. Could you give me a ring? It would be nice to talk. O.K? It's Micky by the way. O.K? Bye.'

Second message:

CLIVE. 'Problems on the distaff side . . . predictably. Sally's just announced she's off to the cinema on Friday evening and as Misha appears to be locked into a permanent state of post-pubescent stupor we have a potential baby-sitting problem. Nothing I can't handle though. Farewell.'

Third message:

EDDIE. ' . . . er . . . hello. This is Eddie. Hope you're well. I'm not. But I'm just phoning to say I'll be there tomorrow (*He yawns. Pause.*) That's it really. (*Off.*) Sue . . . Sue could you pass me my jacket . . . thanks. (*On.*) Right. See you then, then. Tip for the day: never, never mix champagne and vodka. With cocaine. Bye.'

Fourth message:

MICKY. 'Chris, it's Micky again. Look are we on for tomorrow or not? I assume you didn't get my last message, but I really do need to know. I could actually squeeze in a couple of extra Japs you see if we're not. Anyway, give us a ring. It's Micky by the way. Bye.'

Fifth message:

CLIVE. 'Not a great deal of progress to report I'm afraid. The house positively resonates with the sound of heels being dug in. By way of an ante, I foolishly mentioned that tomorrow was no ordinary night . . . the Mother of all Games as it were, but Sally seemed to think that if . . . quote 'it had become that important it was high time we stopped' . . . unquote. Not a logic with which I'm immediately familiar. I seem to be rather the Steve McQueen to her Edward G. Robinson at the moment. Watch this space. Farewell.'

Sixth message:

KEVIN. 'Chris me old matey, it's Kevin here. Bad news I'm afraid. I'm in hospital. (CHRIS *freezes.*) This idiot Reliant Robin would you believe . . . went straight into the side of me on the M.25. I can't remember much about it but apparently the gear stick went straight into my crutch . . . and they're going to have to remove one of my testicles and part of my dick. (*Pause.*) The good news is that it'll get me down to nine and a half stone! Hey!

CHRIS *unfreezes.*

. . . had you going there, didn't I, admit it, just for a moment . . .

CHRIS *fast-forwards to the next message.*

Seventh message:

CLIVE. 'The crisis here has reached positively epic proportions and much as I relish the challenge I have to say my pair of Jacks are looking weaker by the minute. Still there's a good four hours to go. Down but not out. Farewell.'

Eighth message:

MICKY. 'Chris, what the hell is going on? Is it happening tonight or not, I really do need to know. It bloody better be, that's all I can say. Where are you? I've rung your office twice. (*Beat.*) Oh look I'm cancelling the Japs and I'm coming over. Whether there's a game or not. I'll be there at about eight so . . . so . . . there'd better be. It's Micky, by the way.'

Ninth message:

CLIVE. 'This is me circa seven-thirty. (*Beat.*) . . . I'm on my way.'

The doorbell rings. CHRIS *presses the automatic entry.*

MICKY (*off*). Thank God you're in. I called about fifty times.

CHRIS. Three.

MICKY (*entering*). You are expecting me aren't you? I have got the right date?

CHRIS. Of course you have.

MICKY. Thank God for that.

CHRIS. I'm sorry, I've been away a couple of days. I didn't have a chance to get back.

MICKY. It's alright, don't worry about it, you're here. Only I just wasn't sure. I mean tonight of all nights it would have been a bit bloody tragic if we hadn't had a game.

CHRIS. Absolutely. How did it go?

MICKY. You know. What's the plan? Is there anything special lined up?

CHRIS. No.

MICKY. Clive hasn't organised any pranks, then, that I should know about.

CHRIS. Not as far as I know.

MICKY. You would tell me, wouldn't you?

CHRIS. Of course I would.

Pause. MICKY *bursts into tears.* CHRIS *comforts him.*

MICKY. Sorry.

CHRIS. Don't be silly.

MICKY. It was ghastly. Aren't they always? Completely ghastly. The worst thing was . . . I did this. Right in the middle. In fact I keep doing it. He would have hated it. That's a consolation.

CHRIS. Did what?

MICKY. I cried.

CHRIS. That's alright. That's good.

MICKY. It didn't feel good. I mean I know some people discover they love their father after he's died, but I didn't love him before OR after. Or during for that matter. So much so I'm beginning to wonder whether he WAS my father. And then I go and cry at the bloody funeral. I felt so betrayed! By my own body. Like a prostitute having an orgasm. Maybe it was relief. What I wanted was to be completely unmoved so that people would have a glimpse of what a wretched time I'd had. Pure self-pity. Serves me right I suppose. Anyway it's over now. Half of me feels like a grown-up for about the first time in my life which is quite scary, and the other half is doing a kind of crash course in adolescence which is even scarier. Last night I found myself lying in bed worrying about all these cosmic . . . cosmic things that I was supposed to have got out of my system years ago. Like who created God? And why? And when? Do you know what I mean? I don't suppose you do, you're so bloody together, you always have been. The first time I met you you'd just drawn a penis on a picture of God which was about the worst thing anyone could ever think of doing and when you were hauled up in front of the class you defended yourself so eloquently and confidently that I was just so . . . it made me wish I'd done it . . .

Pause.

CHRIS. I drew a penis on a picture of God?

MICKY. Yes.

CHRIS. Are you sure?

MICKY. You were only about eight.

CHRIS. That's rather progressive, isn't it. For an eight-year-old?

MICKY. Not particularly. If you'd really been progressive you'd've drawn a vagina. In fact I'm surprised you didn't. The other thing of course is that I've got to find somewhere else to live. They've put the rent up again. Three times in eighteen months, isn't that illegal? I haven't the faintest clue where to start.

CHRIS. Haven't you been left anything?

MICKY. You must be joking. I was cut out of the will at birth.

Pause.

CHRIS. You can stay here.

MICKY. Here?

CHRIS. Yes. While you're looking.

MICKY. No, no, no I couldn't.

CHRIS. Why not?

MICKY. You don't want me cluttering up your life.

CHRIS. Don't be silly. There's a spare room. It's not that far from your language school. You can write upstairs, I'll write downstairs. I'll be at work most of the time, anyway. At least until you've found somewhere permanent.

MICKY. Are you sure?

CHRIS. Of course.

MICKY. That would be brilliant. Thanks very much. It shouldn't be for that long.

The doorbell rings.

That's brilliant. We can be struggling artists together.

CHRIS *presses automatic entry.*

I'll even decorate the bathroom for you. Since you're never going to get round to it.

KEVIN (*off. Singing*). 'B.A.Y. B.A.Y. B.A.Y. C.I.T.Y.'

He enters, carrying a can of Coke and a McDonald's hamburger.

'With an R.O.L.L.E.R.S. Bay City Rollers are the best.' Team!

CHRIS. Good to see you.

KEVIN. To see you good.

CHRIS. New sweater.

KEVIN. New sweater, new trousers, new shoes, dressed to kill. Funny how some clothes make you look fat, isn't it. (*Tommy Cooper laugh.*) An historic occasion. Did you get my message?

CHRIS. No?

KEVIN. What! I left it on the machine! What a waste! I said that . . . (*Realising he's lying.*) . . . ah, had you worried for a second though, didn't I . . .

CHRIS. No.

KEVIN. Liar.

CHRIS. Not even a milli-second.

KEVIN. Liar!

CHRIS. Reliant Robins aren't allowed on the motorway.

KEVIN. Give that man a coconut. (*Beat.*) Micky, me old matey . . .

He extends his hand to MICKY, *who in turn extends his. At the last second* KEVIN *withdraws his. He chuckles.*

Every time. How are you?

MICKY. Don't ask.

KEVIN. I tell you what.

MICKY. What?

KEVIN. I won't ask. (*To* CHRIS.) Congratulations!

CHRIS. What?

KEVIN. 'What', he says . . . such modesty . . .

MICKY. What for?

KEVIN. You've got a publisher.

CHRIS. Oh. Agent actually.

MICKY. What!

CHRIS. Not a publisher.

MICKY. You've got an agent? Who? How?

CHRIS. Catherine Ellison.

MICKY. Catherine Ellison! She's good. That's wonderful. (*Beat.*) How did you manage that?

CHRIS. Luck really. I just sent in a couple of stories and they liked them. They've asked for more. It'll probably be the kiss of death.

MICKY. No, that's . . . that's wonderful.

CHRIS. Pure luck.

MICKY. Maybe I should switch to stories.

KEVIN. Talking of which, I think it's only fair to warn you, team, that according to my horoscope in the paper this morning, today is going to be financially 'extremely advantageous'. I just thought I'd mention it so that if anyone's feeling a bit short on the old spondulicks . . .

The bell goes.

That'll be the bell.

CHRIS *presses automatic entry.*

Heard about your father, Micky.

MICKY. Oh right. (*Beat.*) Thanks.

EDDIE *enters.*

EDDIE. Itchy fingers. Dryness at the back of the throat. The ever-quickening pulse. It must be that time of the month. And what's more it's the Big One.

KEVIN. Eddie, me old matey, how goes it . . .

EDDIE. Flora margarine? Yes or no?

KEVIN. 'Do you adora Flora?'

EDDIE. Yes?

KEVIN. Yes.

EDDIE. I knew it.

MICKY. Hi, Eddie.

CHRIS. Where is your passenger?

CLIVE (*off*). Here.

CLIVE *enters carrying a bottle of champagne.*

Good evening, gentlemen. Are we in the right place for some male bonding?

CHRIS (*to* CLIVE). You made it. Congratulations.

CLIVE. We have young Steven to thank for the decisive tactic.

CHRIS. What did he do?

CLIVE. Threw up all over me. The fact that it was after a particularly generous plate of spaghetti followed by a swift tutorial on how to do a triple somersault is neither here nor there. Drastic situations call for drastic remedies. Sally is convinced that it's the start of gastroenteritis at LEAST and despite my entreaties to savour the delights of 'Thelma and Louise' refused to leave her sick child. Who am I to contradict the unerring maternal instinct?

CHRIS. You are joking.

CLIVE. I'm here. That's what matters.

EDDIE (*pointing to* KEVIN). Flora margarine. You owe me a tenner.

CLIVE (*handing him the money*). Good God Kevin, is there no end to your talents. I had the misfortune to see you on television last night, playing a particularly repellent policeman.

KEVIN. He wasn't a policeman, he was a private investigator.

MICKY. I saw that. You were very good.

KEVIN. Thanks.

CLIVE. Don't you get fed up always playing policemen?

KEVIN. I don't always. Last year I played a vicar, a test pilot . . .

MICKY. Did you?

KEVIN. A twenty-three-year-old ballet dancer . . .

EDDIE. You don't look anything like a vicar . . .

CLIVE. Ah but that was on radio, was it not.

KEVIN. So?

CLIVE. It does seem to be your niche, the Old Bill. When it comes to the silver screen.

KEVIN. Yeah well, it's not my fault if that's how people see me. Anyway I'm good at it. Shall we start?

EDDIE. Wouldn't you like to play Hamlet?

KEVIN. Only if I could play him as a policeman. (*Tommy Cooper laugh.*)

EDDIE. Seriously.

KEVIN. Not particularly, no.

CLIVE. Why ever not?

KEVIN. I'm afraid of ghosts. (*Tommy Cooper laugh.*) I'm getting my own act together at the moment anyway.

CHRIS. How's it going?

KEVIN. Good.

CLIVE. Consisting of what?

KEVIN. Just a stand-up routine.

CLIVE. Oh try out a few jokes on us, we'll tell you whether you're on the right lines or not.

KEVIN. Thanks Clive, that's very kind of you, but fuck off all the same. Come on let's get started.

CHRIS. Tell us when it happens.

CLIVE. A momentous evening, gentlemen.

CHRIS. Kevin . . .

KEVIN. Sure.

CLIVE. Eighteen years in the saddle for some of us. A coming of age. Eighteen years to the day since the first cards were dealt, way back in the days when men were men and women were women, and half a crown could buy you a packet of Woodbine with change to spare. A fateful evening in the course of which I lost as I recall an entire packet of Opal Fruits and one pound thirty-three in cash. (*Holds up the champagne.*) Cause for celebration I think . . .

CHRIS. I'll put it in the fridge. (*To* EDDIE.) You'd better stay off the vodka and cocaine, Eddie.

EDDIE. What?

CHRIS. How is Sue?

EDDIE. Sue who?

CHRIS. Sue who you were in bed with when you left a message.

EDDIE. Oh Sue! Yes. I had only met her the night before.

CLIVE. One of your lengthier relationships then.

MICKY. The night before?

KEVIN. Take your seats please, team.

They all sit. CHRIS *divides up the chips.* KEVIN *shuffles the cards.*

MICKY. How do you do that?

EDDIE. What?

MICKY. How do you get from meeting a woman who's a total stranger . . . to being in bed with her hours later?

KEVIN. How much?

CHRIS. Fifty each.

MICKY. Not that I particularly want to do it, I just find it intriguing.

CHRIS. Chemistry. Isn't it, Eddie. Pure chemistry.

MICKY. No really, I mean what . . . what words do you use?

EDDIE. It's not just words.

CHRIS. He grunts as well.

EDDIE. You have to fancy each other . . . little signals that you pick up on.

CHRIS. Like salivating.

KEVIN. Me to deal.

CHRIS. And pointing to your crutch.

MICKY. I find it extraordinary.

CHRIS. So do I.

CLIVE. Ignore him, Eddie. I find your approach refreshingly honest. A groin is a groin is a groin. There's nothing more repulsive than when it masquerades as a brain.

KEVIN. Team . . . your attention please . . . this is not the right occasion for petty squabbles and jealousies. What we want is out and out warfare. **Antes in please.**

EDDIE. I've got a proposition to make.

CHRIS. What?

EDDIE. It's controversial.

KEVIN (*as Tommy Cooper*). You want us all to wear petticoats?

EDDIE. No.

KEVIN (*as Tommy Cooper*). YOU want to wear a petticoat?

EDDIE. No.

KEVIN (*as Tommy Cooper*). You want . . .

EDDIE. I want to raise the stakes.

MICKY. Not again.

CLIVE. Why?

EDDIE. There's still not enough muscle. You can't frighten people. Everyone stays in for everything.

KEVIN. So?

EDDIE. Nobody gets hurt enough.

CHRIS. Vetoed.

MICKY. Vetoed.

CLIVE. That seems to be a no.

KEVIN. And they're off . . .

EDDIE. Wimps.

KEVIN. It's that magic moment when opportunity knocks and prosperity beckons. Who knows what the evening will bring, delight or despair, triumph or tantrums, ecstasy, or . . . e . . . e . . .

They all search for a word.

CLIVE. Get on with it.

KEVIN. In other words . . .

The phone starts ringing.

CLIVE. Shit!

KEVIN. That'll be the phone.

EDDIE. Who is it?

CHRIS (*getting up*). I don't know.

CLIVE. Don't answer it.

CHRIS. What?

CLIVE. You heard.

KEVIN. Put the machine on.

CLIVE. Just leave it. (*To* KEVIN.) Deal, will you.

CHRIS. Clive . . .

CLIVE. Just leave it.

CHRIS. Why?

CLIVE. It's for me.

CHRIS. How do you know?

CLIVE. Because I do.

CHRIS. Then you answer it.

CLIVE. Do you want to play poker tonight or not?

CHRIS. Yes.

CLIVE. Well just do me a favour and leave it then.

KEVIN. Put the machine on.

CHRIS. It might be for me or . . .

CLIVE. Oh for Christ's sake . . .

He gets up and answers the phone.

Yes?

Pause.

Yes it is.

He takes the phone outside.

EDDIE. Who is it?

CHRIS. God knows. Sally probably.

He goes over to the door and listens.

KEVIN (*sings in a cod Mexican accent.*) 'Aye, aye, aye, aye . . . ' (MICKY *and* EDDIE *join in.*) . . . Si Si Signora. My sista Beleenda, she peessed out the winda all over my brand new sombrero . . . I said . . . '

CHRIS (*motioning them to be quiet*). It is Sally.

KEVIN. Shit. That's a bad start. Shall I wait?

EDDIE. No.

CHRIS. Yes. I'll open the champagne. Micky, think of a toast.

MICKY. Oh God, do I have to?

EDDIE (*referring to* CLIVE). We could be here all night. Once they get going.

MICKY. I hate doing this kind of thing. Let's think. Er . . .

KEVIN. Oh let's start.

He starts dealing the cards. CHRIS o*pens the champagne and starts to pour.*

EDDIE. Are you in, Clive?

MICKY. How about . . . 'To the last eighteen years.'

There is no answer.

EDDIE. Deal him in. He won't be long.

MICKY. Or the NEXT eighteen years.

KEVIN. Ask him again.

EDDIE. Deal him in . . . that'll get him off.

CLIVE (*off*). Yes, I know . . . of course I realise that . . .

KEVIN. I know.

He finishes the deal.

MICKY. What are we playing?

KEVIN. We're not. Just look as if you are. Clive!

MICKY. I don't understand.

EDDIE *laughs.*

KEVIN. Clive!

CLIVE *sticks his head round the door.*

First hand of the night. Bugger your Neighbour. You've got two Queens, three quid to stay, are you in or out?

CLIVE. **In.**

He exits again.

CHRIS. Guys . . .

KEVIN. Sht. **And they're all in . . .**

CLIVE (*off*). Yes of course I believe you . . .

KEVIN (*dealing*). **And they're off again. Queens meet . . . a bullet . . . Kaspar meets a five . . . Joel meets the king he never wanted . . . dealer takes a nine, looking enigmatic . . .** (*To* CLIVE.) . . . **Queens to bet** . . .

CHRIS. It might be important, you know.

CLIVE *appears again.*

CLIVE (*to the phone*). I DO apppreciate that, I assure you . . . (*To them.*) What?

KEVIN. **Pair of ladies and a bullet.**

EDDIE. **Big pot shaping up**.

CLIVE (*to the phone*). Sorry, I'm just . . . (*To them.*) **I'll match the betting . . .**

KEVIN. **And it's five pounds all round.** (*Deals.*) **Pair of queens meets . . . a THIRD queen . . . remarkable, Kaspar struggles to contend, Joel split down the middle and the dealer hangs on in there with a pair of nines. Pair of nines goes five pounds . . . and they follow . . . what an opener!**

CLIVE (*with his head round the door*). What's happening?

EDDIE. **Fifty odd quid in the pot, you've got three queens.**

CLIVE (*to the phone*). Could you just hold on a second . . . (*To them.*) . . . give me two minutes, I'll be with you in two minutes . . .

KEVIN. Two minutes!

CLIVE (*to the phone*). Look are you . . . (*To them.*) **Raise it the maximum and match whatever else goes in . . .** (*To the phone.*) What did you say?

He stays in the room.

KEVIN. **And they're all there for the duration. And now the moment the crowd have all been waiting for . . . the final card . . . could it be an Ace for the three Queens or even the fourth Lady, only one person can tell us . . .**

EDDIE. But he's still on the telephone . . .

KEVIN. **Three Queens to speak . . .**

CLIVE (*to the phone*). Listen we'll talk tomorrow, yes? No, I can't. Not now.

KEVIN. With the world at his feet . . .

CLIVE (*to the phone*). Yes alright . . . I said yes, didn't I? Alright. Goodbye.

He puts the phone down. KEVIN *and* EDDIE *enjoy a private celebration.*

Jesus, Joseph and Mary what is happening to my life. Thank you all for being so unhelpful.

MICKY. Everything alright?

CLIVE. No.

EDDIE. I thought we were very patient.

CLIVE (*to* CHRIS). For the record, I blame you. Right, what's happening?

He stares at his cards.

Three Queens. Where are they? You said I had three Queens.

EDDIE *and* KEVIN *start laughing.*

Oh I see. I'm afraid that's not very funny.

EDDIE. Kevin's idea.

KEVIN. We thought you needed a bit of help getting off the phone.

CLIVE. How thoughtful.

KEVIN. It seemed to work anyway.

CLIVE. Yes, well as I say, I think it was FUCKING unfunny.

Silence.

KEVIN. Clive . . .

EDDIE. It was a joke . . .

KEVIN. Yes . . . it was only a bit of fun.

MICKY. We didn't actually put any money in.

CLIVE. So is that what I should tell Sally when I get back tonight. 'Sorry I couldn't continue that row with you earlier this evening darling but the boys were having a bit of a joke.'

KEVIN. I'm sorry. I'm really sorry. I had no idea.

CLIVE. No. (*Beat.*) But I did.

Pause. KEVIN *gathers the cards.*

CHRIS. Is Steven alright?

CLIVE. Steven's fine. (*Beat.*) Steven's always been fine.

CHRIS. Ah.

CLIVE. Precisely. She says if I'm not back in the next half hour she's leaving. I think that's what's called an ultimatum. Give us a drink, will you.

CHRIS. It's champagne.

CLIVE. So?

CHRIS *pours him a drink.*

EDDIE. What are you going to do?

CLIVE. Stay here, of course.

CHRIS. That doesn't sound like a terribly good idea to me.

CLIVE. Well it's none of your business, is it.

CHRIS. Don't you think it might . . .

CLIVE. No I don't.

Pause. They look at him.

It's alright. She's bluffing.

KEVIN *passes him the cards. He deals in silence. The lights fade.*

When they go back up again, it is the Present. CHRIS *is on his own, packing.* EDDIE *enters.*

EDDIE. Is Clive not back yet?

CHRIS. No. He's obviously buying the entire off-licence. Are you feeling any better?

EDDIE. Yes thanks. I'm sorry about that. It rather took me by surprise.

CLIVE. You're not the only one.

EDDIE. I got the worst of it off.

Pause.

The finger seems a bit better anyway.

CHRIS. Good.

Pause.

EDDIE. I mentioned the table to Clive and he reckoned you could definitely get it out. Something to do with turning the legs the other way, I didn't quite understand. (*Beat.*) I suppose he's used to it. Shifting paintings around all the time. (*Beat.*) Only paintings don't have legs, do they.

Pause.

What next?

CHRIS. The box by the fridge.

EDDIE *goes to the box, picks it up and is about to go out when he puts it down on the table instead.*

EDDIE. Chris . . .

CHRIS. Yes?

EDDIE. I don't know how this happened but it has and . . . basically I'm in a bit of a situation.

CHRIS. What kind of situation?

EDDIE. I know it's no good me wishing I could turn the clocks back, but just this once . . .

CHRIS. Are we talking money or women?

Pause.

Or both?

EDDIE. Women. Woman, rather.

CHRIS. Go on.

EDDIE. No, this one's serious. Really serious.

CHRIS. Don't do it then.

EDDIE. It's a bit late for that actually.

Pause.

CHRIS. Are you sure you want to tell me?

EDDIE. Of course I don't want to tell you. I have to. (*Beat.*) It involves Clive and stuff he was talking about earlier on . . .

CHRIS. Clive?

EDDIE. Yes.

Pause.

CHRIS. Oh my God.

EDDIE. It's bad.

CHRIS. I don't want to hear.

EDDIE. Chris . . .

CHRIS. I do NOT want to hear. (*He picks up a box.*)

EDDIE. Chris . . .

CHRIS. I mean it!

> CHRIS *exits, carrying the box.* EDDIE *is left on his own for a moment.* CHRIS *re-enters.*
>
> The thing is that somewhere, deep down, at a blissfully subconscious level, I knew it. I knew it already. Just the way he spoke and the way you listened.

EDDIE. Christ. Was it that obvious?

CHRIS. In retrospect, rushing out of the room and vomiting all over the front-door was a bit of a give-away, yes.

EDDIE. To Clive as well?

CHRIS. God knows, the state he's in. What the hell do you think you're doing?

EDDIE. It wasn't planned or premeditated. It was a comfort thing. She's in such a mess at the moment. She's desperately unhappy.

CHRIS. Oh, so you thought a quick fuck would cheer her up.

EDDIE. Chris, I'm looking for help here, not abuse.

CHRIS. Well you've come to the wrong person then.

> CLIVE *enters with a bag from the off-licence. He hands* CHRIS *his keys.*

CLIVE. I must say a quick fuck would cheer ME up no end. You know I'm delighted you're moving if for no other reason than I won't have to return to that despicable little off-licence. It's a complete and utter rip-off and they seem to think that if they smile a lot it won't matter. There you are.

> *He hands* CHRIS *a carton of guava-juice.*

CHRIS. Thanks.

CLIVE. I was thinking on the way back that if I was the terminally jealous kind or in an episode of *Cracker* or whatever, I'd pin a map of London to the wall, draw a red line showing the bus route of the number 73, nick Sally's address book, stick a pin in every place that's got an address and see who's closest. And then hire someone to kill them both. Or do it myself.

CHRIS. Clive, I really am very very sorry.

EDDIE. Yes.

Pause.

CHRIS. Let's get some supper, shall we . . .

CLIVE (*taking out his bottle of whisky*). Where do you think I've just been?

EDDIE. I don't think I'm up to eating just yet.

CHRIS. I need to get out.

EDDIE. Kevin might turn up.

CLIVE. What about that pub where I persuaded Micky those girls were coming back to play strip-poker? (*To* EDDIE.) And he pitched up instead.

EDDIE. Don't say it like that.

CHRIS. Alright.

EDDIE. You were all pretty relieved at the time, as I remember.

CLIVE. I'll write a note for Kevin.

Silence as CLIVE *scribbles a note.*

CHRIS. I wish they HAD come.

CLIVE. Who?

CHRIS. Those women.

CLIVE. They didn't strike me as being the poker-playing type.

CHRIS. I don't mean THEM, necessarily. Any women. We should have had women in the game.

CLIVE. Why?

CHRIS. It might have been different.

CLIVE. It certainly would have been.

CHRIS. For all of us.

EDDIE. How come?

CHRIS. Including Micky.

EDDIE. How come?

CHRIS. He might still be alive!

CLIVE (*Beat.*) If Newton hadn't been looking when the apple fell we wouldn't all be floating around six feet off the ground, would we. Come on, I'm thirsty.

He exits.

CHRIS. You stupid prick!

EDDIE. Chris, I know what I've done. Do you think he knows?

CHRIS. Of course he doesn't. Why do you think all your limbs are still intact.

EDDIE. Oh don't say things like that. I don't need anyone to make me feel any shittier than I already feel.

CHRIS. Where do you draw the line, Eddie. You personally. Or does the line not exist? You've just gone to bed with Clive's wife . . . CLIVE! who you've been friends with for twenty years, who you travelled halfway round the world with, who . . .

EDDIE. Daughter.

CHRIS. What?

EDDIE. Daughter. Not wife.

CLIVE (*off*). Come on!

Silence. The door opens. CLIVE *sticks his head round.*

Are you two coming or not?

EDDIE. Sure.

He exits.

CLIVE. Are you alright?

CHRIS. Yes. I'm fine.

They exit. Blackout.

End of Act One.

ACT TWO

The same as the last scene in Act One only an hour or two later. The room is emptier. CLIVE *and* CHRIS *are carrying the table, trying to manoeuvre it through the door.* EDDIE *watches them, rolling a cigarette.*

CLIVE. Plastic beams. It actually had black plastic beams! They've completely ruined it.

CHRIS. Up a bit.

CLIVE. Do they think we're very very stupid? I mean do they expect us not to notice that everything's made of plastic and somehow actually believe that we're sitting in a pub that's four centuries old, or do they just expect us not to mind? Either way it's a fucking insult and somebody should let them know.

CHRIS. I think somebody did. Let's try the other way round.

CLIVE. It's the same at work. People pitch up with some piece of drivel that would shame a four-year-old, tell me it's a Titian they've found in their attic and expect me to ejaculate on the spot.

EDDIE. You're wasting your time.

CLIVE. I'm inclined to agree.

CHRIS. You're the one who said if I turned the legs round it would go.

EDDIE. It wasn't me, it was him.

CHRIS. Come on, it's nearly there! Up a bit. And down.

CLIVE. Which?

CHRIS. Up, then down.

They struggle for a bit unsuccessfully. CLIVE *stops.*

What's the matter?

CLIVE. Whisky please, Eddie?

EDDIE. What?

CLIVE. I need some whisky to assist me through this entirely pointless excercise.

CHRIS. It's almost there.

CLIVE. It's not even nearly there.

> EDDIE *brings his glass.* CLIVE *drinks, while holding the table.*

> Thank you. You see it's very simple really, Chris. The table is bigger than the doorway. Or to put it another way, the doorway is smaller than the table. Either way you choose to look at it, the fucking thing won't fit, so I suggest we put it down before I do myself, you and probably the table some serious injury.

CHRIS. But it came in! It definitely came in!

EDDIE. How?

CHRIS. I don't know. I can't remember.

CLIVE. Well maybe it's grown since it's been here, the fact is you're not going to get it out.

CHRIS. Put it down then. Just put it down.

CLIVE. Willingly.

> *They put it down. Pause.*

> Why don't you just leave it here?

EDDIE. Yes, give it to the next people.

CLIVE. Exactly. There. A helpful, if uncharacteristically generous suggestion from young Eddie.

EDDIE. I'm very generous!

CLIVE. Only with your sperm.

> *Pause.*

EDDIE. No I just meant . . . at least you wouldn't have to chop its legs off or something drastic like that.

CLIVE. Do they know about Micky?

CHRIS. Who?

CLIVE. The next people.

CHRIS. I shouldn't think so. It wasn't exactly a selling point. It's a couple. The estate agent said they were going to knock most of the walls down and paint the entire place pink.

EDDIE. They DID know about Micky then?

CHRIS (*beat*). That's a really stupid thing to say.

EDDIE. It was just a joke.

CHRIS. It's the kind of thing he had to put up with all the time when he was alive and it wasn't very funny then. Now that he's dead, maybe you could give it a break.

CLIVE. Well he was gay wasn't he?

CHRIS. Was he?

CLIVE. I imagine so. (*Beat.*) In spite of rumours to the contrary.

EDDIE. What rumours?

CLIVE. Well apparently it has emerged that Micky signed off with a bit of a flourish. He spent his last day . . .

CHRIS. Drop it, Clive.

CLIVE. It may not be true.

CHRIS. Just drop it.

Pause.

I don't know whether Micky was gay or not. I don't suppose he did. It doesn't strike me as being particularly relevant; but when people make remarks like that it makes me realise that they obviously didn't like him very much.

EDDIE. I liked him a lot.

CLIVE. So did I. He was hard not to like. I just didn't like the bit of him that happened to be gay.

CHRIS. Unfortunately you can't divide people up into their separate components like that, discarding the bits you don't happen to like, you've been playing too much Lego with Steven. So Micky might have been gay. Why does it have to matter so much?

CLIVE. It doesn't. I just didn't like it. I don't like it. The idea of two men having sex together disgusts me.

CHRIS. I'll assume it's the drink.

CLIVE. It's not the drink, it's me. I'm not going to stop them or beat them up in some dark alley. But I wouldn't want to do it myself, I wouldn't want my son to do it and from time to time I permit myself the occasional puerile joke about it.

CHRIS. Only 'cos you're afraid of it.

CLIVE. I'm not in the least bit afraid of it. I don't like it. I really think I should have the right to not like something.

CHRIS. Well you could at least try!

CLIVE. Try? Do you mean pretend?

Silence. CHRIS *starts packing up a box.*

CHRIS. I think we should give Kevin a ring.

CLIVE (*moving to the phone*). I'll do it.

EDDIE. He's definitely coming.

CLIVE. Oh Jesus!

EDDIE. What?

CLIVE. I've left my address book behind.

EDDIE. Where?

CLIVE. In that Godforsaken pub.

EDDIE. It'll still be there.

CHRIS. If they let you in.

CLIVE. They will. Or I'll set fire to the plastic.

CHRIS. Why don't you leave it and pick it up later.

EDDIE. I should get it now. You never know.

CLIVE. Yes. I won't be long.

He exits. Pause.

CHRIS. He really can be very objectionable sometimes. He never used to be.

CHRIS *continues packing.*

EDDIE. We need to talk.

CHRIS. Do we?

EDDIE. I need advice.

CHRIS. Well it takes about five minutes to get to that pub and back so you'd better be quick. I'm just hoping against hope that there's a part of my brain that's malfunctioning today and that although I keep hearing things I don't want to hear, in actual fact they're not being said. (*Beat.*) You are having an affair with Misha?

EDDIE. No.

CHRIS. Thank God for that! It is me.

EDDIE. I wouldn't call it an affair.

CHRIS. What would you call it?

EDDIE. It was just one night.

CHRIS. Oh no . . .

EDDIE. Months ago. Not even a night, an evening. A . . . one-evening stand. I mean we hardly did it.

CHRIS. 'Hardly'? Either you did or you didn't.

EDDIE. We did. But it was very quick.

CHRIS. Great. What are you going to tell me next, you didn't put it all the way in?

Pause.

EDDIE. Listen, I did it because . . .

CHRIS. I know why you did it! What I don't know is why you didn't NOT do it.

EDDIE. Same difference, isn't it?

CHRIS. Why did you have to pick her, for God's sake?

EDDIE. I didn't pick her. I told you it wasn't planned. It was the day I helped move some of Sally's stuff out in the van. Clive didn't want anything to do with it so Misha gave me a hand and . . . well, we got talking and she obviously wanted help. She's not as brave or as grown-up as she seems, you know. Anyway we stopped off and had a drink on the way back, at my place. And she talked. About Clive and her stepmother and everything that was going on and . . . and . . . I saw no harm in that and then we drank a bit more . . . quite a lot more in fact and I think we even smoked a bit and then . . . I hadn't PLANNED anything, obviously . . . but she asked me to hold her and it just kind of went on from there. Neither of us really knew what we were doing. Maybe she did, maybe it was her way of getting at Clive, she's pretty shrewd, you know.

CHRIS. Eddie, she is seventeen years' old. You said it yourself.

EDDIE. Sixteen. (*Beat.*) I told you it was a comfort thing.

CHRIS. Bollocks. You did it because apart from anything else you love doing it. You love being ABOUT to do it. You love wondering whether it's going to happen. And you love it when it does happen.

EDDIE. Yes, alright. I love women.

CHRIS. Sex, not women.

EDDIE. I love sex AND women. Don't you? It is possible to like both, you know.

CHRIS. I'm beginning to wonder. Did it not occur to you that she might be screwed up enough as it is?

EDDIE. I don't think you're being very helpful.

CHRIS. I'm depressed, that's why. At the effect this might have on Misha. Not to mention Clive. I'm depressed that for just once in your prick-driven life, you weren't able to forget your 'instincts' or your 'conditioning' or whatever else it is that makes you feel you have to fuck everything that moves and just say 'no'!

EDDIE. Oh and I suppose you're always saying 'no' . . .

Silence. CHRIS *turns away.*

It was a one-off, a mistake. I thought it was all over and done with . . . and then she pitched up out of the blue last week, wanting to . . . I didn't really give her a chance to say what she wanted, I just said I thought we should go back to how it was before. She got all upset and tearful and then it all got a bit nasty and ended up with her threatening to tell Sally and Clive. (*Beat.*) Look, I know it's not exactly . . . according to Hoyle but it's happened. I needed to tell someone, that's all. I needed to tell you. (*Beat.*) Hello?

CHRIS. Does anyone else know?

EDDIE. Only Kevin. Kind of. Christ, every morning for the last week I've woken up with a bellyful of fish-hooks.

CHRIS. Yes. Well, they won't go away in a hurry.

Pause.

EDDIE. So it wasn't THAT obvious.

CHRIS. Does it matter?

EDDIE. Yes it does rather.

CHRIS. You know what you have to do.

EDDIE. What?

CHRIS. Tell him.

EDDIE. I can't do that. You've seen how he is at the moment. He'll kill me.

CHRIS. Tell him.

EDDIE. No.

CHRIS. Then I'll tell him.

EDDIE. You can't.

CHRIS. Yes I can.

EDDIE. Why!

CHRIS. Because there are some secrets that are best left secret and there are some that are not.

EDDIE. Oh you mean like other people's!

The doorbell rings. CHRIS *presses the automatic entry.*

Please, Chris. Please?

They stand looking at each other. Blackout.

The lights go back up in their alternative state. It is a year on from the previous past scene. MICKY, KEVIN and CLIVE are seated round the table. KEVIN shuffles. MICKY smokes a herbal cigarette.

MICKY. Omar Sharif?

KEVIN. Yes.

MICKY. You're really going to be filming a commercial with Omar Sharif?

KEVIN. Yes.

MICKY. How exciting. (*Beat.*) I thought he was dead.

CLIVE. It'll be a pretty tasteless commercial if he is.

KEVIN *deals.*

KEVIN. It's high, it's low, but above all . . . it's mean . . . it's none other than . . . **Montana Red Dog** . . .

He lets out a wolf-howl.

CLIVE (*calling*). Eddie!

EDDIE (*off*). Coming.

KEVIN. **And it's a four to the dealer's left, followed closely by a bullet, then comes a one-eyed boy, dealer bringing up the rear with a suicidal king. Bullet to speak.**

MICKY. What is it for?

KEVIN. It's just a commercial. **Bullet to speak.**

MICKY. **Check.**

EDDIE *enters inhaling deeply from a small tin.*

CLIVE. It's your bet.

KEVIN. What's that?

EDDIE. Floor-polish. I haven't had this for about ten years.

He inhales again.

MICKY. What does it do?

EDDIE. It polishes floors. (*Beat.*) Oh I see. It just speeds up the old brain a little bit.

CLIVE. You could have fooled me.

MICKY. Where did you get it from?

EDDIE. Upstairs. It's alright, I'm not going to sniff it all. Have some.

EDDIE *offers it to* MICKY.

MICKY. No thank you.

CLIVE. Certainly not. It's your bet.

EDDIE. Kevin?

KEVIN. No thanks.

EDDIE. What's the matter with everyone? Good clean fun. **Check.**

KEVIN. Chris is taking his time isn't he?

EDDIE. He's found some woman. I bet you anything.

MICKY *reacts.*

What?

MICKY. It's a book launch not a brothel.

EDDIE. How much? Ten? Twenty?

MICKY. No.

EDDIE. Go on, if you're so sure. Fifteen, split the difference.

MICKY. Alright.

EDDIE. Done.

KEVIN. Why weren't we invited?

MICKY. I was. I didn't feel like it.

CLIVE. I keep seeing his face beaming down at me from various posters on the way to work. It really is excruciating. In fact I've taken to scrawling little Hitleresque moustaches on them as a way of coping.

He bets a pound.

KEVIN. **A pound from the big King, says he's got one underneath. Do they believe him?**

They all bet.

No, they don't.

MICKY. It's not a very good picture, is it.

CLIVE. What?

MICKY. On the poster. It's not a very good likeness.

CLIVE. It isn't by the time I've finished with it.

KEVIN deals again.

MICKY (*to* EDDIE). Kevin's doing a commercial with Omar Sharif.

EDDIE. Are you? I thought he was dead.

KEVIN. He's not.

EDDIE. He's a nancy-boy, isn't he.

KEVIN. Omar Sharif!

EDDIE. Yeah. He plays bridge. At least he used to.

KEVIN. **The four meets the curse of Scotland, the bullet snuggles up to an eight, boy meets boy, the suicidal king meets a miserable seven, still in with a chance. Boys to bet, commands respect.**

EDDIE (*bets*). **Two.**

KEVIN. **Two to compete. Dealer stays. Four nine . . . follows and raises! Looking good for the low.**

MICKY *hesitates.*

Hesitation on my left.

CLIVE. You don't have any whisky, by any chance, do you?

MICKY. Top cupboard on the right.

KEVIN. **I'll have to hurry you.**

EDDIE *makes a chicken noise.*

MICKY. I'm thinking.

KEVIN. Go on Micky, take a risk for once in your life.

EDDIE. You scratched your nose when you raised it.

CLIVE. Did I?

EDDIE. Yes.

CLIVE. Fascinating.

EDDIE. Why?

CLIVE. I had an itch.

EDDIE. Either because you were bluffing.

KEVIN. He is. (*To* MICKY.) Come on!

CLIVE. You mean I was PRETENDING to have an itch.

EDDIE. Or . . . because you weren't.

CLIVE. A characteristically brilliant observation, if I may say so Eddie. If that's the level of insight you're going to bring to the game, then we're in for a truly awesome evening.

KEVIN (*sings*) 'Aye, aye, aye, aye . . . '

MICKY. Oh no . . .

KEVIN (*the others join in*) 'Si, si Signora . . . '

MICKY. I haven't been that long . . .

ALL. 'My seesta Beleenda she peessed out the weenda, all over my brand new sombrero. I said you twat, you peessed on my hat, and she said I don't fucking care-o.'

    MICKY bets.

KEVIN. Too late, you're out.

MICKY. I was in. I've just bet!

KEVIN. Too late.

EDDIE. He was in.

CLIVE. Got good cards, have you Eddie . . .

MICKY. I was in I promise you. I bet on the 'c' of 'care-o'!

KEVIN. Team?

CLIVE. Close, but I think he gets the benefit of the doubt.

EDDIE. Yeah.

MICKY. Thank you.

    The others bet in sequence.

KEVIN. **And they're all in. The crowd go mad! And the four nine is joined by a lady, spoiling the low, the bullet eight meets royalty, and he's in all sorts of difficulties, the pair of boys find a handsome seven and the king seven enigmatic with a lovely looking four. Pair of boys.**

    Starting with EDDIE, each of them knocks on the table in turn. We hear the front door open.

KEVIN. **And it's a clear round. Last cards.**

    He deals. CHRIS enters.

CHRIS. Sorry I'm late everyone. I got away as soon as I could.

MICKY. How was it?

CHRIS. Brilliant. It went really well.

MICKY. Good.

CHRIS. I'm half-pissed I'm afraid.

CLIVE. Excellent. We'll deal you in.

MICKY. It went on a long time.

CHRIS. Yes.

EDDIE. Did you meet meet anyone?

CHRIS. I met lots of people.

EDDIE. Anyone . . . special?

CHRIS (*ignoring him*). Who's winning?

EDDIE. Well, did you?

CHRIS. That's not what I was there for.

EDDIE. See? He did.

MICKY. Excuse me, but we are in the middle of a hand. Eddie to bet.

EDDIE. **Boys check to the fours.**

KEVIN. May the fours be with you. **Five pounds.**

CLIVE. **Fold.**

MICKY. **And five.** There's some supper in the oven. It's probably a bit burnt by now.

CHRIS. I've eaten. They had the most amazing spread. Deal me in the next hand will you.

He exits.

KEVIN. And it's time to change. Micky? **Loses the bullet and pulls a five.**

MICKY. I don't suppose anyone else wants a burnt Fray Bentos steak and kidney pie do they?

KEVIN. Yeah go on, I'll get rid of it for you. Eddie? **Loses a boy but pairs his three!**

CLIVE gets up and tries to unlock the garden door.

MICKY. Where are you going?

CLIVE. For a leak. If I can open this door.

MICKY. I'd rather you didn't. (*Beat.*) I'm serious.

CLIVE. You're smoking a herbal cigarette. Nothing you say or do can be serious.

MICKY. There is a toilet upstairs.

CLIVE. There's also a garden outside.

MICKY. Into which I've just put some bedding plants.

CLIVE. I'm going for a leak. Not a crap. It's a question of tradition you see, Micky.

MICKY. Why?

CLIVE. It doesn't matter why.

EDDIE. Chris won't mind.

MICKY. Well I do and seeing as how I've spent the best part of a year now getting that garden into shape I'd rather you used the toilet. I don't think I'm being unreasonable. (*To the others.*) Am I? Given that it's 1994 and he's a grown man, is it unreasonable to expect him to use a toilet?

KEVIN. I'm with you, Micky.

CLIVE. What is it with this gardening business? Is it genetic? One moment you're a perfectly normal human being and then some chromosome snaps into place and bang! You wake up the next morning babbling about herbaceous borders.

KEVIN. Are we playing poker or what? **It's seven to stay.**

CLIVE. Thank God it hasn't happened to me.

CHRIS *enters.*

Sorry to plunge you into the real world again quite so abruptly, but do you have any objections to my urinating in your garden? I can't imagine why you would, I've urinated in most other places in your house.

MICKY. Not since I've been living here.

CLIVE. Well?

CHRIS (*beat*). Is the toilet broken?

CLIVE. No.

CHRIS (*beat*). I'm not even sure I know where the key to that door is.

CLIVE. Oh look if you're going to sit on the fence, sit on it. Don't ponce around deciding which BIT of it you're going to sit on.

CHRIS. Alright then . . . no, I'd rather you didn't.

Pause. CLIVE *moves to the door.*

CLIVE. You sounded horribly like my second wife then.

He exits.

CHRIS. Did I miss something there?

EDDIE. Sally's moving out.

CHRIS. Oh God. Definitely?

EDDIE. When rather than whether.

MICKY. Can we just finish this hand without any more interruptions please.

KEVIN. It's your bet.

CHRIS. I'm surprised she's lasted this long.

MICKY. Call.

EDDIE. Fold.

KEVIN. **Declarations please Gentlemen. On the count of three. One, a-two, a-three.**

MICKY and KEVIN *hold their clenched fists over the table. On the count of three, they open them. They both have a chip in their hand.*

EDDIE. **And they've both gone high.**

KEVIN. **Ten pounds.**

MICKY. **Call.**

KEVIN. **Two pairs, kings on sevens.**

MICKY. Shit. Shit. Shit. **Queens on eights.**

KEVIN. Yes!

MICKY. Look at that. I've had second-best cards all night. All year.

KEVIN. It's not the cards that matter. It's the situations.

MICKY. Well I've had second-best situations as well.

EDDIE. If I'd been able to bet more I'd have frightened him out.

KEVIN. Here we go.

EDDIE. It's true.

CHRIS (*to* MICKY). Everything alright here? No calls?

MICKY. No.

CHRIS (*giving him a present*). Happy Birthday.

MICKY. Oh. Thanks.

KEVIN. Is it your birthday?

MICKY. Last week.

KEVIN. You should have told us.

EDDIE. Yeah.

KEVIN. We would have . . . we would have . . .

EDDIE. We would have known. How old are you?

MICKY. Don't ask.

KEVIN. I tell you what . . .

MICKY. What?

KEVIN. I won't ask. (*Tommy Cooper laugh.*)

MICKY *has unwrapped a mug.*

MICKY. Great.

CHRIS. It's got a frog inside.

MICKY. Oh right. Thanks for the warning. So it went well.

CHRIS. Brilliant. Champagne on tap and a room full of people all telling me how clever I am.

MICKY. Yuk.

CHRIS. I left feeling about eight foot tall.

Pause.

MICKY. So DID you meet anyone?

CHRIS. As it happens . . .

EDDIE. I told you . . .

CHRIS. I met an extremely nice woman called Clare, an editor and . . . we got on rather well. I'm seeing her again next week.

EDDIE (*to* MICKY). Fifteen, let's have it.

CHRIS. How could you know it? How could you possibly have known it?

EDDIE. I just did.

CHRIS. How!

EDDIE. The way you . . . (*Beat.*)

CHRIS. What?

EDDIE. It's alright. You are allowed to fancy people aren't you? What's her name again?

MICKY. Kevin's got a job.

CHRIS. Clare. What?

MICKY. Kevin's doing a commercial with Omar Sharif.

CHRIS. Are you? Excellent.

CLIVE (*entering*). What's it for, this commercial of yours?

KEVIN. Money.

CLIVE. No, really.

KEVIN. Fish. Since you ask.

EDDIE. What kind of fish?

KEVIN. Just fish, you know, that you eat. Gills, fins, little round eyes.

EDDIE. What do you have to do?

KEVIN. Team, it's just a commercial.

CLIVE. But you and Mr Sharif must both have to do something?

KEVIN. Yeah I play the hero and he plays the fat ugly git. (*Tommy Cooper laugh.*) I'm a seal. Since you ask.

MICKY. A seal!

CLIVE. A police seal, presumably.

EDDIE. Do you have to wear a seal costume?

KEVIN. Yes. Well not exactly. You don't really want to know all this . . .

CLIVE. Yes we do.

EDDIE. What happens?

KEVIN. It's three human seals sitting on a drum by a pool dressed a bit like Dick Van Dyke and the seals in 'Mary Poppins'.

MICKY. Penguins.

KEVIN. What?

MICKY. They're penguins, not seals.

KEVIN. Are they?

CLIVE. He's right.

KEVIN. That's it, really.

CHRIS. What do you have to wear to look like a penguin?

KEVIN. White shirts and black trousers down by your knees. Only we're not having shirts because we're not penguins, we're seals.

EDDIE. Topless seals.

MICKY. What happens?

KEVIN. What happens . . . team . . . do you really want to know?

ALL. Yes.

KEVIN. There are half a dozen of us standing around dressed like seals. Omar comes on . . .

CHRIS. Christian names already . . .

KEVIN. Omar comes on and throws us each a fish . . . which we catch in our mouth and a voice says something about . . . the ultimate SEAL of approval or something like that.

CHRIS. Inspired.

KEVIN. Isn't it.

MICKY. How do you catch a fish in your mouth?

KEVIN. God knows.

EDDIE. That's impossible.

CHRIS. I hope they're paying you well.

EDDIE. Quite impossible.

KEVIN. Can we get on with the game now, or . . .

CLIVE. So if I chuck a peanut up in the air, you should be able to catch it.

EDDIE. Easy.

CLIVE *throws a peanut at him. He ignores it.*

KEVIN. Clive . . .

CHRIS. You're too close.

EDDIE. Up on the chair then, go on up on the chair.

KEVIN. Team, please.

CHRIS. We want a preview.

CLIVE. You won't be able to do it on the day . . .

EDDIE. You need all the practice you can get.

CHRIS. Up on the chair.

KEVIN. Guys, is this really necessary?

CLIVE. Up on the chair.

KEVIN. I get vertigo.

ALL (*singing*). We want Kev the penguin, we want Kev the penguin, we want Kev the penguin . . .

KEVIN. I'm a SEAL.

ALL. We want Kev the seal, we want Kev the seal . . .

EDDIE. Up on the chair!

KEVIN. Alright, alright I'll tell you what I'll do.

CHRIS. What?

KEVIN. I'll get up on the chair. (*Tommy Cooper laugh.*)

They cheer as he climbs up.

By popular demand . . .

EDDIE. Get your kit off!

CLIVE. Trousers down.

KEVIN. No! Absolutely not.

CHRIS. The future of the British Fish Industry could depend on you.

KEVIN (*as Tommy Cooper*). I tell you what I'll do.

CHRIS. What?

KEVIN (*as Tommy Cooper*). I'll keep my trousers on.

EDDIE. Come on!

KEVIN (*holding on to them. As Tommy Cooper*). Just like that.

CLIVE. If you can't drop them in front of us you'll never manage it in front of Omar.

KEVIN. My knees'll get cold.

EDDIE. Get 'em off!

CHRIS. I'll do the fish. How far back do I have to stand?

CLIVE. By the door.

MICKY. Nearer than that, give him a chance.

CHRIS. On the count of three . . .

EDDIE. It's not the same with the trousers on.

KEVIN (*pulling them down an inch or two. As Tommy Cooper*). Any more and I'll be arrested. (*Tommy Cooper laugh.*)

They begin drumming on the table.

ALL. A-one, a-two, a-three!

EDDIE *throws a peanut.* KEVIN *snaps at it and misses. They boo.*

KEVIN. Stop that! (*As Tommy Cooper.*) Yes Sir, which way did it go?

CLIVE. And another!

CHRIS *throws again and* KEVIN *misses. They boo again.*

KEVIN (*as Tommy Cooper*). Has he thrown it yet?

EDDIE. Rubbish! Get him off!

CHRIS *begins to throw a steady stream of peanuts at* KEVIN *who tries desperately to catch them. Meanwhile* EDDIE *creeps up behind him and suddenly yanks his trousers to his knees.* KEVIN *quickly tries to retrieve them. There is a great cheer that fizzles out as they glimpse that* KEVIN *is wearing a pair of women's silk knickers. He pulls his trousers up. An awkward silence.*

MICKY. Did you manage to catch any?

KEVIN. No.

EDDIE. Useless.

KEVIN. It'll be easier with a fish. (*Beat.*) I expect.

Pause. CHRIS *drops to his hands and knees.*

EDDIE. What are you doing?

CHRIS. There's peanuts all over the floor.

EDDIE. I'll give you a hand.

MICKY. What does Tilly think?

KEVIN. About what?

MICKY. This commercial.

KEVIN. She thinks it's great. Good money.

CLIVE. I hope you don't mind my asking but . . . do you always wear women's underwear?

Pause.

KEVIN. How do you mean?

CLIVE. It's just that I couldn't help noticing you were wearing a pair of women's knickers.

KEVIN. I'm not.

CLIVE. I think you'll find if you look again . . . you are.

KEVIN. I think I should know what kind of underpants I'm wearing.

CLIVE. I agree with you there. What does anyone else think?

Pause.

MICKY. Er . . .

EDDIE. They were a bit . . . colourful.

CHRIS. Let's get back to the cards, shall we.

CLIVE. I'm intrigued. Take them down again, let's have another look.

KEVIN. I'm not taking my trousers down again, take your own down.

CLIVE. I could, only it won't really solve the mystery.

KEVIN. There's no mystery *to* solve. Can we get on with the game?

They take their places round the table again.

MICKY. Whose deal is it?

CHRIS. Mine, I think.

Pause.

For what it's worth . . . I thought Omar Sharif was dead.

Pause. They look at him.

What?

KEVIN. Just deal, will you?

He deals in silence. The lights fade.

They come up again on CHRIS *and* EDDIE *standing facing the door as we previously left them. It is the present.* CLIVE *stands in front of them, carrying his address book.*

CLIVE. I've seen Micky. I swear to God I've just seen Micky.

CHRIS. Where?

CLIVE. It was quite uncanny. I went into the pub, got the address book, and as I was on my way back I saw this little figure walking along the road, hugging the wall, you know the way Micky always used to hug the wall in case the world tipped over and he'd have nothing to hang onto, so I waited for a moment and as he passed me he looked up and it was him! The hair, the eyes, the mouth . . . everything. He was even smoking one of those revolting herbal cigarettes. I was just about to say something when I realised it was rather foolish. Does that ever happen to you?

CHRIS. All the time.

Pause.

EDDIE. No trouble at the pub?

CLIVE. It was disappointingly uneventful. I was looking forward to at least a minor fracas. How are your guts?

EDDIE. Alright thanks. For the moment.

CLIVE. Good.

Pause.

Maybe it WAS Micky. Maybe he's come back to haunt us. As some kind of revenge for not taking him seriously enough.

CHRIS. Speak for yourself.

CLIVE. I was speaking for all of us actually. Not everyone has the decency to announce their own suicide.

CHRIS. He didn't.

CLIVE. Only for it to fall on deaf ears.

CHRIS. It was a manner of speech, not a real threat.

CLIVE. Except that it was.

Pause.

EDDIE. Kevin reckons he was a virgin.

CLIVE. He was when we last saw him.

EDDIE. It makes sense, doesn't it. (*To* CHRIS.) You always said that if he could only have found someone . . .

CHRIS (*trying to put some things into a box*). Give us a hand with this, will you Clive.

EDDIE (*Beat.*) What do you mean 'when we last saw him'?

CLIVE. What?

CHRIS. I'm supposed to be out of here on Monday.

EDDIE. He was a virgin 'when we last saw him'.

CLIVE. If this rumour is to be believed.

CHRIS. Clive . . .

CLIVE. We are all grown-ups now, you know. Well . . . nearly all of us. According to some friend of his sister's, when they went through the clothes he'd been wearing that night, some sharp-eyed copper found one of those little cards you find in telephone booths, stuck in his top pocket. It looks like Micky spent his last day . . . and I imagine his life savings . . . with a prostitute.

Pause.

EDDIE. You're joking.

CLIVE. Male or female I do not know.

EDDIE. Micky?

CLIVE. It may not even be true.

CHRIS. Female. And it is true.

CLIVE. How do you know?

Pause.

CHRIS. Because it wasn't a copper who found it. It was me.

CLIVE. You! And you never told anyone? Like us?

CHRIS. Only his sister.

EDDIE. What about the police?

CHRIS. I didn't think it was a good idea. For Micky or for his family. For anyone.

EDDIE. But something could have happened that might explain . . .

CHRIS. Nothing happened. (*Beat.*) I went to see her. About a week later. Just to see what kind of state he'd been in. Of course she didn't want to speak. It didn't occur to me she might not remember who he was. Or might not WANT to. I should have taken a photograph. It didn't matter in the end though. I paid her. And described him, and she knew straight away. She said normally they all blur into one, but she remembered him, not because of anything special that happened, but because . . . just because he cried when he came. And kept on crying.

Pause.

EDDIE. Micky. And a prostitute.

CLIVE. A final fling before going to meet his Maker.

EDDIE. So he stormed out, spent the next day with some hooker and then came back here. What did he bother to come back for? Why didn't he . . .

CHRIS. I don't know! I never spoke to him again, so how the fuck should I know!

Pause.

CLIVE. I don't think Eddie was suggesting that you HAD spoken to him again.

CHRIS. Then why does he go on about it? Nobody knows why he went off or why he came back, nobody really knows why he did it . . . nobody knows anything so why waste time inventing possibilities. He was unhappy, more unhappy than any of us guessed . . . that's all we know. Maybe he didn't mean to do it but he did. Can't that be enough? Or do we have to keep digging around?

Pause.

CLIVE. You should have moved straightaway.

CHRIS. Yes.

The doorbell rings.

EDDIE. About bloody time.

He presses the automatic entry.

CLIVE. Looking on the bright side . . .

He moves to the garden door.

. . . at least I can urinate in the garden in relative peace.

He exits.

KEVIN (*off.* SINGING) 'B.A.Y. B.A.Y. B.A.Y.C.I.T.Y. with an R.O.L.L.E.R.S . . . Bay City Rollers are the best.'

KEVIN *enters carrying a large suitcase.*

Team! The thriller in Manila. The confrontation this worldwide audience has been eagerly anticipating for the best part of two decades. The Final Game.

EDDIE. Here.

KEVIN. Here.

EDDIE. You're late.

KEVIN. Chris, me old matey, how are you?

They shake hands. KEVIN *pulls his hand away at the last second.*

Every time. (*To* EDDIE.) YOU . . . are in trouble.

EDDIE. What?

KEVIN (*indicating* CHRIS). Have you . . .?

EDDIE. Yes.

KEVIN. The wheel has finally come off, my son.

EDDIE. What are you talking about?

KEVIN. Misha phoned. Left a message.

CLIVE *enters unnoticed.*

EDDIE. Kevin . . .

KEVIN. Wanting to find out where you were. Sally's trying to get hold of you urgently. And I mean URGENTLY.

CLIVE. Who?

CHRIS. What's with the suitcase?

KEVIN. What? (*Beat.*) Oh hi, Clive.

CLIVE. Hello.

Pause.

KEVIN (*to* CHRIS). I'm working round the corner tonight so I thought I'd change here. (*Beat.*) Saves having to go home in between.

CHRIS. Right. What are you doing?

KEVIN. I'm trying out some stand-up.

CHRIS. You're actually performing?

KEVIN. Only fifteen minutes.

CHRIS. You kept that quiet. You said you'd let us know.

KEVIN. Yeah, well. (*Beat.*) Sorry I'm late by the way. Looks like you've got most of it done. Good timing.

CLIVE. So Sally phoned you, did she?

KEVIN. No. I mean . . . sorry, yes. Yes she did.

CLIVE. With a message for . . .?

KEVIN (*Beat.*) You.

CLIVE. For me?

KEVIN. Yes.

CLIVE. Only you weren't looking at me.

KEVIN. When?

CLIVE. When you said there was a message.

KEVIN. Wasn't I? Well you don't always, do you.

CLIVE. What?

KEVIN. Look at someone when you're talking to them! Jesus!

Pause.

CLIVE. Well?

KEVIN. What!

CLIVE. What's the message?

KEVIN. Oh. She said . . . she was having trouble getting through to you . . . and . . . something to do with the phone . . . and . . . she just wanted a chat really, nothing urgent . . . in fact, I shouldn't . . . she said not to bother getting back. (*Beat.*) She just thought you might be round at my place. Before coming on here.

Silence.

CHRIS. Gentlemen, now we are four, shall we . . . (*Indicates the table.*) . . . assume the position.

KEVIN. Oh you've already started. What's the state of play?

EDDIE. I'm a little behind.

CHRIS. Clive's soared into an early lead.

Silence as they sit round the table and CHRIS *sorts the chips and cards.*

KEVIN. It looks a little bare in here doesn't it. (*Beat.*) Are you nervous?

CHRIS. About what?

KEVIN. Getting married!

CHRIS. Only because people keep asking me whether I am. I was perfectly alright till then. Now I feel I OUGHT to be. (*To* CLIVE.) Were you nervous?

CLIVE. What?

CHRIS. When you got married. The first time. Were you nervous?

Pause.

EDDIE. I would be.

Pause.

KEVIN. And it's Clive to deal.

EDDIE. How much have we got?

CHRIS. Fifty quid. (*To* KEVIN.) So where are you performing?

KEVIN. Just round the corner. A new place.

CHRIS. Why didn't you warn us?

CLIVE (*dealing*). **Indian.**

KEVIN. Indian! For the opening hand. Unprecedented. And the crowd go mad.

They each place a solitary card on their forehead.

EDDIE. Kevin to bet.

KEVIN. **Unimpressed by the opposition. He goes a bold fifty pence.**

CHRIS. **Call.**

EDDIE. **Up a pound.**

CLIVE. **And another.**

KEVIN. **So cruel, so young.**

CHRIS. **Your bet.**

KEVIN. **Call.**

CHRIS. **Call.**

EDDIE. **Up five.**

CHRIS. **Three pound limit.**

EDDIE. Oh come on . . .

CHRIS. Half the pot, that's the rule.

EDDIE. **Up three.**

CLIVE. **Another three.**

KEVIN. **Call and two.**

CHRIS (*dropping his card*). No way, José.

KEVIN. The first casualty. Good decision.

EDDIE. **His three, your two and four.**

KEVIN. When the going gets tough, the tough get going.

CLIVE. **Call and another four.**

KEVIN. **At which point** (*Putting his card down.*) **. . . he reluctantly but gracefully bows out.** Three of clubs. Probably the worst card in the world.

EDDIE. **Always nice to shake off the stragglers. Your four and another five.**

KEVIN. **He's confident.**

CLIVE. **Five.**

EDDIE. **Yes.**

CLIVE. **Fifty.**

KEVIN. **Fifty pence, beginning to crack.**

CLIVE. **Pounds.**

> *They laugh.*

> I mean it.

EDDIE. Fifty pounds.

CLIVE. Yes.

CHRIS. I think you'll find that's over the limit.

CLIVE. That's up to Eddie.

EDDIE (*laughs. Pause*). What's going on?

CLIVE. Is fifty pounds too much for you? You're always complaining that the stakes are too low, aren't you? That you can't fuck people about enough, so here's your chance. No limit poker. Fifty pounds to kick off.

CHRIS. I don't think you can do that, Clive.

CLIVE. I'm not playing with you, I'm playing with Eddie. Don't tell me you're going to say no?

EDDIE. For real?

CLIVE. Yes.

EDDIE (*Beat.*) Alright, whatever you say . . . fifty quid.

CLIVE. Put it in, then.

> EDDIE *takes the money out of his wallet and puts it in the pot.*

How much are you raising it?

EDDIE. I'm not.

CLIVE. Why on earth not? This is no-limit poker, you can do what the hell you like!

> *Pause.*

EDDIE. I don't want to.

CLIVE. I'd have thought it would be a dream come true for a little scumbag like you.

> *Silence.*

It doesn't have to be cash. I'll accept material goods if that's any help . . . your guitar, your stereo . . . whatever. So what are you going to raise it?

EDDIE. I've told you, I'm not.

CLIVE. Why not?

EDDIE. I don't want to play any more.

CLIVE. 'I don't want to play any more.' You little shit.

KEVIN. Team . . .

CLIVE. You know what really disgusts me . . . what turns my stomach . . . is not the betrayal but the deception. It's not what you've done but the fact that for the past God knows how long, every time we've met or sat at this table, you've been lying to me. Repeatedly and shamelessly lying to me, asking me how I am, how things are, how Sally is . . . and all the while you've been fucking her behind my back.

EDDIE. Clive . . .

CHRIS. Oh Jesus . . .

CLIVE. How long HAS it been going on as a matter of interest . . . Weeks? Months? Not that I give a damn about what she gets up to . . .

EDDIE. I haven't done anything with Sally.

CLIVE. Eddie you may have noticed that I've been surprisingly calm about all this so far, but I warn you now if you start playing games with me and tell me ONE MORE LIE I will tear your fucking legs off.

CHRIS. I don't think this is the best way . . .

CLIVE. What are you defending him for?

CHRIS. I'm not defending anyone.

CLIVE. Oh no! That's not what it sounds like.

KEVIN. I think you're making a lot of assumptions.

CLIVE. You keep out of this, this is none of your business. Except that you must have known as well. Did you? Either of you?

CHRIS. This is crazy.

CLIVE. Kevin?

KEVIN. What?

CLIVE. Unbelievable. Nobody is capable of giving me a straight answer to a perfectly straight question.

EDDIE. I have not done anything with Sally. Ever.

CLIVE *launches himself at* EDDIE.

CLIVE. DON'T BLOODY LIE TO ME!

EDDIE. I'm not. Tell him for God's sake!

CHRIS *and* KEVIN *try to restrain him.*

CHRIS. Clive, get off him.

KEVIN. Come on matey.

CLIVE. I'VE PLAYED POKER WITH HIM FOR TWENTY YEARS, DO YOU REALLY THINK I CAN'T TELL WHEN HE'S LYING. HE HAS THE GALL TO RUN AROUND WITH MY WIFE BEHIND MY BACK BUT HE HASN'T GOT THE BALLS TO COME OUT AND SAY IT TO ME!

EDDIE. Get him off for God's sake!

CHRIS. Leave him alone Clive . . .

EDDIE. I SWEAR TO GOD I HAVE NEVER SET A FINGER ON SALLY AND SHE HAS NEVER SET A FINGER ON ME. Now will you please let go of me.

CLIVE *stops. He releases* EDDIE. *Silence.*

CLIVE (*to* CHRIS). Is he telling the truth? I can't tell any more. Just tell me either way and I'll believe you. Is he telling the truth?

CHRIS. Yes.

CLIVE. You promise?

CHRIS. Yes.

CLIVE. Because if you're covering up for him . . .

CHRIS. I promise.

Pause. CLIVE *cries.*

CLIVE. Oh shit. Oh shit! I'm sorry. Eddie I am so sorry. It's just . . . third time round, if I thought there was no hope . . . I don't know what I'd do. I love her so much. And I treat her like shit. Forgive me, please.

EDDIE. Of course.

CLIVE *hugs him.* CHRIS *and* KEVIN *watch on.*

CLIVE. That's better. (*To* ALL.) Sorry about that. Slight overload on the old circuit board. (*Beat.*) I suspect I've rather screwed up the betting on that hand, let's see, there's about . . . what . . . thirty pounds in there . . . of which, who . . . who was in at the end?

He breaks down again. This is the crying of someone who has not cried for a long time. CHRIS *comforts him.*

CHRIS. Clive, I think it would be a good idea if you went home.

CLIVE. Yes. I think you're probably right. As ever. I don't think I'd survive a game of poker just at the moment. I'm sorry to let you down.

KEVIN. Don't be silly.

CHRIS. Will you be alright getting back?

CLIVE. Yes, yes.

KEVIN *hands him his coat.*

CLIVE. Thanks.

Pause.

I do apologise.

CHRIS. Don't be absurd.

CLIVE. Thanks. I'll see you soon then.

He exits. Silence.

CHRIS. I feel grubby.

EDDIE. I've never seen Clive cry before.

CHRIS. Really grubby.

EDDIE. I didn't know he could.

> KEVIN *picks up the cards from the floor.*

KEVIN. I think these are shuffled. (*Tommy Cooper laugh.*)

EDDIE (*picking up a card from the table*). Was that my card? A king? Bloody hell.

> *Pause.*

> Thanks, guys.

CHRIS. What for?

EDDIE. For not telling him.

CHRIS. I think you'd better leave as well.

EDDIE. He doesn't know. He still doesn't know.

CHRIS. Just go, will you.

EDDIE. Where?

CHRIS. Anywhere. Home. I don't know, just go!

> *He gets his coat.*

> Christ, if my hands are still shaking like this when I play tonight I'll drop the guitar.

> *Pause.*

> Pity about the game. Another time. See you.

> *He exits. Pause.*

KEVIN (*holds up the cards*). Snap? Beggar my neighbour? Happy Families?

> *Pause.*

> I might as well get changed.

> KEVIN *exits. The lights fade on* CHRIS.

> *When they come up again he is sat at the table with* EDDIE, KEVIN, CLIVE *and* MICKY. *They are in the middle of a hand. It is one month on from the previous past scene.*

EDDIE. First of all I was NOT doing eighty-five and I don't care what their bloody machines say . . .

KEVIN. **Five.**

CLIVE. **Call.**

EDDIE. In any case that van is incapable of doing more than seventy . . . **call** . . . secondly I had had precisely two pints of beer and that's a fact, so that's another piece of police technology that's up the spout and thirdly I did NOT spit at the Arresting Officer, I sneezed. Surely they know the difference between a sneeze and a spit.

CHRIS. **Up five**.

MICKY. **Call.**

EDDIE. I mean, why would I want to spit at a policeman? I've got better things to do with my saliva . . . like swallowing it.

KEVIN. **And ten.**

CLIVE. **Call.**

KEVIN. Are you alright, Micky?

MICKY *nods.*

EDDIE. **Call.** Apart from anything else, I was standing about ten yards away from him at the time. Johnny Rotten with the wind behind him wouldn't have managed that.

CHRIS. **Call.** Any witnesses?

EDDIE. No.

MICKY. **Fold.**

CLIVE. And the men being separated from the women.

EDDIE. If I lose my licence . . . I bet you . . . it won't be because of speeding or drinking, but because some piece of fluff floated up my nose at the wrong place at the wrong time.

CHRIS. When are you in court?

EDDIE. I don't know yet.

CHRIS. I can't promise anything, but I'll see what I can do.

EDDIE. How am I supposed to get to gigs without the van? That's my livelihood.

CLIVE. Oh shit.

EDDIE. It's a nightmare. A bloody nightmare.

CLIVE. I was going to ask you to move some of Sally's stuff.

EDDIE. I was there for six hours. Six hours! (*Beat.*) Move it where?

CLIVE. Out.

EDDIE. Oh right. I thought she'd already gone.

CLIVE. She has. Her personal belongings haven't.

EDDIE. Well, if I've still got the van.

CLIVE. Make sure he gets off, will you? You don't happen to have any more of this nectar do you?

CHRIS. No, sorry.

MICKY. Yes we have. In the cellar. You put it there just before the game, remember? I'll get it.

Beat. MICKY *gets up and goes out.*

CLIVE. Would I be right in thinking Micky's suffering from a severe case of P.M.T?

CHRIS. He's been like that for a while. (*Beat.*) I asked him to move out.

CLIVE. Ah.

CHRIS. Not immediately. But as soon as he could find somewhere else. Don't say anything, will you.

MICKY *enters and hands* CLIVE *a bottle of whisky.*

CLIVE. Thank you very much.

Silence. EDDIE *deals each of them another card.*

So. You're being booted out, are you Micky? That's the trouble with these bastard landlords. I'd offer you a room in my own house now that there's a vacancy . . . but I have to say I'm still rather savouring the rediscovered delights of bachelordom. **Ten in.**

EDDIE. **No.**

CHRIS. **No.**

KEVIN. **Too much.**

CLIVE. **All mine?**

CHRIS. **All yours.**

CLIVE. I eat what I like. When I like. I wash when I like. If I like. In fact it really is rather alarming to see how quickly one reverts. Do you know I'd ordered a take-away pizza within three minutes of her leaving the house? Four season, thin crust, I didn't even have to look at the menu. Remarkable stuff, D.N.A.

MICKY. I've shuffled them.

CHRIS. Where's she gone?

CLIVE. Oh, some ghastly friend of hers.

MICKY. I said I've shuffled them.

CHRIS. I'm sorry. I didn't hear.

CLIVE. One of those nazi feminists who believes all men should be marinaded in their own urine. Of course that would probably turn you on.

KEVIN. Steven's gone as well, has he?

CLIVE. Yes. (*Beat.*) The next phase is to entertain hordes of loose women at every available opportunity. Though the ever-present Misha rather queers the pitch in that particular department. If I could farm her out to HER mum, I'd be laughing.

CHRIS *deals.*

KEVIN. So is Clare moving in here?

CHRIS. Yes.

KEVIN. That's a bit quick isn't it? You've only known her six weeks.

MICKY. Four.

KEVIN. It must be the L word.

EDDIE. Lust.

CLIVE (*to* MICKY). What are you going to do?

MICKY. I don't know. Ask Chris.

CHRIS. **Cincinnati. King showing.**

MICKY. **Check.**

KEVIN. **Two.**

CLIVE. **Call.**

EDDIE. **Call.**

CLIVE. Chris, what's Micky going . . .

CHRIS. What most people do I expect. **And two.**

MICKY. **Call.**

KEVIN. **Call.**

CLIVE. **Call.**

EDDIE. **Call.**

CHRIS (*dealing*). Look in all the usual places. **King and a ten showing.**

MICKY *reacts.*

CHRIS. What?

MICKY. Never mind. **Check.**

KEVIN. **Check.**

CLIVE. **Check.**

CHRIS. **Ten.** (*To* MICKY.) What!

MICKY. You are just so . . . feckless sometimes.

CHRIS. Feckless?

MICKY. Yes. Completely and utterly devoid of any . . . any . . .

KEVIN. Fecks. (*Tommy Cooper laugh.*)

CLIVE. Your bet, Micky.

MICKY. **Ten and ten.**

KEVIN. **Big spender.** (*Beat.*) And he folds.

CLIVE. **Me too I'm afraid**.

EDDIE. **Call.**

CHRIS. **Call and another ten.**

> *The game has now got rather tense. Pause.*

MICKY. **Call.**

KEVIN. **He calls!**

CLIVE. **He must know something we don't.**

EDDIE. **I'm out.**

> CHRIS *deals another card to* MICKY *and himself.*

> I might need a character witness.

KEVIN. What for?

EDDIE. If I go to court. Any offers?

MICKY. **Check.**

KEVIN. What does it involve?

EDDIE. You just have to turn up and say what a good bloke I am.

CHRIS. **Ten.**

> *Pause.*

EDDIE. Well don't all rush to volunteer, will you.

CLIVE. I'll do it. Perjury's one of my strengths.

EDDIE. Thank you.

MICKY. **Call.**

CHRIS (*he deals*). **And it's a seven.**

CLIVE. Micky, I hope you don't mind my asking but why are you still in this hand, Chris has been betting like a maniac since the first . . .

MICKY. That came off the bottom.

CHRIS (*beat*). What did?

MICKY. That card. It came off the bottom of the pack.

Silence.

CHRIS. Micky it did not come off . . .

MICKY. I'm sorry I saw it! Someone else must have noticed, surely?

Pause.

EDDIE. I wasn't paying too much attention actually.

KEVIN. No.

CHRIS. I dealt it the way I've been dealing all night.

MICKY. Well in that case they've all been coming off the bottom because I definitely saw where it came from.

CHRIS. Don't be silly, Micky.

MICKY. Don't call me silly. I'm not a five-year-old.

Pause.

CLIVE. I think it's highly unlikely that Chris would have deliberately dealt off the bottom.

MICKY. Why?

CLIVE. Why?

MICKY. Yes.

CLIVE. Because, much as it hurts me to say it to his face, Chris is an honest fellow who is not in the habit of . . .

MICKY. Oh that's great, and where does that leave me? Everybody take Chris's side. Chris is right because Chris is always right and everything he touches turns to fucking gold. Which means that I must be a little liar and if I'm such a little liar then I can't be worth playing with can I, so fuck that and fuck all of you. I might as well throw myself under the nearest fucking bus. Fuck, fuck, fuck.

He throws down his cards and storms out. Silence.

CLIVE. With that she flounced out.

EDDIE. What was all that about?

CLIVE. The man's mad.

KEVIN (*getting up*). Do you think he's alright? Maybe I should go after him.

The front door slams.

EDDIE. He's left the house.

KEVIN. I'll get him back.

CHRIS. I'll go.

KEVIN. No, you wait here.

EDDIE. What about the game?

KEVIN *exits. Pause.*

Did you see the state of him?

CHRIS. What the hell am I supposed to do? End my relationship just so Micky can have a roof over his head? He was only ever meant to be here for a few weeks or months at the longest. It's been great but I need the space now. Anyone would think I'd asked him to shoot his own grandmother.

Pause. He gets up.

I think I'd better go after him as well . . .

EDDIE. No . . .

CLIVE. There's no point everyone going after him.

CHRIS. But I'm the one he's angry with.

EDDIE. He looked pretty angry with everyone, actually.

CLIVE. Just sit down and let Kevin sort it out. Believe me, I've had two children, I know about these matters.

Pause.

EDDIE. He had a little bit of froth coming out of his mouth. He hasn't been bitten by a dog recently has he?

CHRIS. I'd just like to say that I did not deal off the bottom.

EDDIE. I didn't see you do anything wrong. But then I wasn't really paying attention.

CHRIS. Thanks.

EDDIE. No, I'm just saying.

CLIVE. I certainly didn't notice anything at the time but thinking back now there were a number of rather furtive hand movements . . .

CHRIS. Yeah, yeah. I wouldn't know how to, apart from anything else.

EDDIE. I thought he was going to hit you.

CHRIS. I told you he'd been odd the last few days.

CLIVE. Micky has always been odd.

CHRIS. He hasn't.

CLIVE. The man is barking.

EDDIE. That wasn't odd. More like homicidal.

CHRIS. He's a very loyal friend.

CLIVE. Loyal or not he's barking. Give him a padded cell and a bean-bag, he'd be happy as Larry. What are you doing?

CHRIS (*collecting the cards*). Well we're not playing on, are we?

EDDIE. Why not?

CHRIS. Micky's gone, Kevin's disappeared . . .

EDDIE. He'll be back.

CHRIS. When?

EDDIE. When he's found Micky.

CHRIS. IF he finds Micky. We don't know how long that'll be. It's already late.

CLIVE. It's midnight.

CHRIS. Not after that. I don't feel like it.

EDDIE. Don't take it so personally.

CHRIS. I'm the one he accused of cheating!

Pause.

CLIVE. What are we supposed to do between now and dawn?

EDDIE. Yeah. We could have a three-hander.

CHRIS. Look I really don't feel like it. I'm sorry!

Pause.

EDDIE. I don't know why we bother any more.

CHRIS. I should have gone after him.

CLIVE. Come on, Eddie. Let's go and get hideously drunk somewhere.

EDDIE. You already are.

EDDIE *and* CLIVE *get ready to leave.*

CLIVE. All I can say is that Micky has a lot to answer for. Or you, for that matter. There will of course have to be a formal inquiry.

CHRIS. I did NOT deal off the bottom.

EDDIE. What about the next one then . . . three weeks today? Assuming Kevin's found Micky by then.

CHRIS (*looking through his diary*). Friday the eleventh . . .

EDDIE. We'll be there.

CHRIS. Is Clare's birthday.

CLIVE. So?

CHRIS. We're going out. To celebrate.

CLIVE. Can't you go out on the Saturday?

CHRIS. Her birthday isn't on the Saturday.

EDDIE. Pretend.

CHRIS. Pretend what?

EDDIE. That it is.

CHRIS. I think she knows what day her birthday is.

CLIVE. You might not.

CHRIS. I do.

CLIVE. But you might not. Just get it wrong. You haven't known her very long, it's not entirely implausible. She might even find it rather endearing.

CHRIS. The answer is no.

CLIVE. Why not?

CHRIS. Because it's unpleasant, selfish and deceitful.

CLIVE. Yes, but apart from that why not?

CHRIS. No. (*Beat.*) We could PLAY on the Saturday.

CLIVE. Don't be ridiculous. It would be like going to church on a Monday.

CHRIS. Can't YOU pretend? (*Beat.*) How about the second Friday after that?

CLIVE. Yes I'm sure she'll settle for that. After all what's a birthday at our . . .

CHRIS. To play!

EDDIE. O.K. with me.

CLIVE. If you insist.

CHRIS. I'll tell Kevin. And Micky.

EDDIE (*to* CLIVE). All set?

CLIVE. Do you think we can trust him to settle up Eddie? Or is that a little rash in view of tonight's events.

EDDIE. See you, Chris.

CHRIS. Bye.

CLIVE. Five weeks. Five whole weeks. Farewell.

They exit. CHRIS *clears the cards. The lights fade.*

They come up again on CHRIS *in the 'Present'. The room is now virtually empty. He checks all the cupboards one by one until he discovers one that he has missed.*

CHRIS. Shit!

He looks around for a box. There are none.

KEVIN (*off*). Chris.

CHRIS. Yes.

Pause.

KEVIN (*off*). Nothing.

CHRIS (*beat.*) Everything alright?

KEVIN (*off*). Yes.

CHRIS. Are you ever coming out of there?

He goes out and returns with a large, half-full cardboard box. He puts it on the floor by the cupboard, opens it up and stops for a second as he sees something inside. He begins to empty the cupboard into the box. KEVIN *enters. He is dressed as a woman.*

Jesus!

KEVIN. What do you think?

CHRIS. You look . . . What's the idea?

KEVIN. What do you think?

CHRIS. Is it drag night or something?

KEVIN. No. But I thought I'd liven things up a bit.

CHRIS. You look extraordinary. Give us a twirl.

KEVIN turns.

No wonder you took so long. It's great. I love it.

KEVIN. It's silk. Pure silk. I found it in this second-hand shop. I told them it was for Tilly.

CHRIS. What the hell do you do in this act?

KEVIN. Tell a few stories, the odd joke. I'm just me, really. (*Beat.*) It's different though, isn't it.

CHRIS. It certainly is. What do you call yourself?

KEVIN. Kevin.

CHRIS (*beat*). Right.

Pause.

KEVIN. When you say 'extraordinary', what do you mean exactly?

CHRIS. Well . . . exactly that. Out of the ordinary. Don't you get hot under that wig?

KEVIN. A bit.

CHRIS. What does it feel like?

KEVIN. Good. Really good.

He laughs a long uninhibited laugh that is entirely his own.

CHRIS. Have you tried it before? Dressing up?

KEVIN. You mean in front of people? Not quite like this, no.

CHRIS. Tilly?

KEVIN. Tilly what?

CHRIS. You've tried it out in front of Tilly.

KEVIN. No. One step at a time.

Pause.

CHRIS. It's quite hard to have an ordinary conversation with you like that.

KEVIN. Why?

CHRIS. It just is.

Pause.

KEVIN. So you're all packed, are you?

CHRIS. Just about.

KEVIN. I don't suppose we'll be playing again, will we?

CHRIS. Not here.

KEVIN. Not anywhere.

CHRIS. It doesn't look like it.

KEVIN. It's never been the same since Micky.

CHRIS. No.

Pause.

Sorry I can't help staring.

KEVIN. I haven't turned into a different person. If women can wear trousers I don't see why I shouldn't wear a dress.

CHRIS. Sure.

Pause.

KEVIN. You know what I heard the other day?

CHRIS. What?

KEVIN. There's a story going round that Micky spent the last . . .

CHRIS. Yes, yes I know.

KEVIN. Oh.

CHRIS. So much for secrecy.

KEVIN. Only I kept thinking of him as I was getting changed just now. I could almost see him lying in that bath. You see it so often in films, don't you. The water turning red and all that. Horrible. It probably wasn't like that at all.

CHRIS. It was.

Pause.

KEVIN. So is it true? The story.

CHRIS *nods.*

CHRIS. That's where I see him now. In a grubby loveless bedsit. A man with tatoos listening at the door. Micky heaving away at some strange woman's flesh. She hating Micky, Micky hating her. But most of all Micky hating himself. Not the ideal circumstances in which to lose your virginity, are they?

Long silence.

KEVIN. I must make a move.

CHRIS. You're early.

KEVIN. I'll have a drink.

CHRIS. Or six.

KEVIN. I'm not nervous. Not as nervous as I was walking in here. (*Beat.*) This time tomorrow I'll have done a voice-over for Heineken lager and arrested John Thaw. (*He laughs.*)

CHRIS. Don't forget to take your lipstick off.

KEVIN (*pointing to the last box*). Sure you don't need a hand with that?

CHRIS. No. No don't worry. You don't want to ladder your stocking.

KEVIN. How could I ladder my stocking carrying a box?

CHRIS. It was just a joke.

Pause.

KEVIN. I'll get my case.

As he exits, snap light change and MICKY *appears. It is several hours on from the previous past scene.*

CHRIS. Micky . . . where the hell have you been?

MICKY. I'm so sorry. I'm so terribly sorry.

CHRIS. It's two o'clock. I've been worried.

MICKY. Have you?

CHRIS. You look terrible. Kevin went after you but said you'd just disappeared. Where have you been?

MICKY. Nowhere in particular. Just wandering around. I needed to get out.

CHRIS. Are you alright?

MICKY. Yes.

CHRIS. Are you sure?

MICKY. Yes.

Pause.

Who won?

CHRIS. No one. We stopped.

Pause.

MICKY. I'm finding the game a bit of a struggle at the moment. What with Clive and . . . everyone really. It used to be such fun. But now it's as if you're all speaking a different language. (*Pause.*) I'm so sorry for saying those things. Will you forgive me? You weren't cheating, well you know that, but I somehow managed to convince myself that you were. I was just so angry. Everything's been bottled up for so long and there's so much trying to get out, little bits of me are getting trampled to death in the stampede. And suddenly for some reason I thought it was all your fault. Which is quite irrational 'cos it isn't. You've been a very good friend.

CHRIS. I should have given you more warning about Clare. It doesn't give you much time.

Pause.

MICKY. Were you really worried about me?

CHRIS. Yes!

MICKY. What time is it?

CHRIS. Two o'clock.

MICKY. I don't feel remotely tired.

CHRIS. Would you like a drink or something?

MICKY. No.

Pause.

CHRIS. Do you want to talk?

MICKY. What about?

CHRIS. Anything.

MICKY. No.

Silence.

Do you realise I've been teaching English to Japanese businessmen for sixteen years now. That's almost half my life. It was only a four-week contract when I started. Then six months, then a year . . . just to buy time to write. Only now, SIXTEEN years later, although the entire population of Tokyo speaks perfect English, I'm still only on page a hundred and twenty-three of the same novel. That's what . . . seven pages a year? Talk about a long labour, more like a stillbirth. (*Beat.*) And worst of all at the age of thirty-six . . . (*Pause.*) I sometimes wonder whether something terrible didn't happen to me as a kid, which I've sort of instinctively forgotten or repressed. I expect I'm going to find out pretty soon. I don't mean being dropped on my head or . . . strangled by the umbilical chord or anything traditional like that . . . though I suppose it could be . . . but I mean something REALLY terrible like . . . like . . . I don't know . . . so terrible I can't even think of it. The sort of thing that if I COULD remember I wouldn't be so screwed up. It's probably on its way up even as I speak . . . it'll pop out one afternoon in Tesco's in the form of green bile like that girl in *The Exorcist.* I kind of hoped that it being the end of the Millennium, not just the decade or the century but the MILLENNIUM . . . that the next few years would be a bit like a . . . like a kind of doormat on the threshold of a new era where everyone . . . me included . . . me ESPECIALLY . . . could wipe off the bits of the past that have got stuck to the bottom of their shoes, the bits they don't like, the bits that screw them up and then everything would be alright, you know I could . . . I could actually meet someone and . . . (*Pause.*) But I'm not sure if I can wait that long. (*Long pause.*) Chris . . . I realise that this isn't exactly according to Hoyle but . . . would you mind awfully if I spend the night with you?

CHRIS (*beat*). How do you mean?

MICKY. I mean I don't want to . . . I'm not going to jump on top of you or anything, not if you don't want me to . . . I'm not gay, at least (*Laughs.*) I say that . . . but maybe I am . . . I'm not ANYTHING as far as I know . . . but it would be nice *to* know. (*Beat.*) Do you think?

CHRIS. I'm still not entirely clear what you're asking.

MICKY. Nor am I.

Pause.

I do need to be close to someone. Just for tonight. If only for comfort's sake. And it would be nice if it was you.

Pause.

CHRIS. When you say 'close' what exactly . . .

MICKY. Christ this is a nightmare do I really have to spell it out . . .

Pause.

Oh dear. I know that look. Somewhere between pity and revulsion. My father used it rather a lot.

CHRIS. I'm sorry. To be honest with you, I don't think it's a great idea. I'm not sure I could handle it.

MICKY. Right. Shit. Forget about it. I just didn't . . . don't want to spend the night on my own.

CHRIS. Sure. I understand that. Listen, why don't you bring your mattress into my bedroom and stick it down on the floor somewhere. (*Beat.*) Or I could bring mine up to you if you prefer.

MICKY. That's not quite what I meant.

Pause.

It's alright. It doesn't matter.

Pause.

Well. That was a bit of a conversation-stopper, wasn't it? Even by my standards.

CHRIS. You do understand, don't you?

MICKY. Yes. Absolutely.

CHRIS. I mean if there's anything else . . .

MICKY. Don't worry about it.

Pause.

I think I'll call it a day now.

CHRIS. There's nothing else you want to talk about?

MICKY. No.

CHRIS. Sure?

MICKY. Quite sure. Night night.

CHRIS. Night.

MICKY *exits. The front door slams.*

Micky . . .

He gets up and goes to the door.

Micky!

Snap light change. KEVIN *enters with his suitcase. The Present.* CHRIS *is still staring after* MICKY.

KEVIN. What's up?

CHRIS. Oh nothing.

KEVIN. You shouted 'Micky'.

CHRIS. Did I?

Pause.

KEVIN. I'll see you on the big day. If not before.

CHRIS. Right.

KEVIN. Tell me . . . what's she like?

CHRIS. Who?

KEVIN. Clare. I've never met her.

CHRIS. What!

KEVIN. I've always been ill or away working or on holiday. I have never met her.

CHRIS. I didn't realise.

KEVIN. So what's she like?

CHRIS. Well she's . . . she's . . . lovely. She's intelligent and . . . she's got a fantastic arse. (*Beat.*) But maybe not in that order. Good luck for tonight.

KEVIN. Thanks.

He exits. CHRIS *contemplates the table. He looks at the doorway. He up-ends the table so that the legs are sticking up into the air. He goes over to the last remaining box, opens the lid and takes out a saw. He returns to the table. The lights fade on him as he starts sawing off the first leg.*

The End.

Glossary

'High Low' games Games in which players can choose to go for either the highest or the lowest hands in order to win.

Declarationsville The point at which players have to indicate whether they are high or low or both. This is done when everyone places either none (low), one (high) or two (both) chips in their hand and then opens their fist simultaneously.

Ante A small compulsory bet at the start of a hand that buys you the right to participate.

The Flop Anything from three to ten cards placed in the middle which when turned up are common to everyone's hand.

The Curse of Scotland The Nine of Diamonds.

Paddy Any eight (after Mr Ashdown . . . neither high nor low).

A Bullet An Ace.

Suicidal King The King of Hearts who unlike any other King appears to have a sword through his head.

One eyed Jacks The two Jacks who can only be seen in profile.

Boys Jacks.

Ladies Queens.

The Games

Mexican Sweat. Seven cards to each player all face down. The first player turns up a single card. The following player then has to turn up as many cards as it takes to beat the first player . . . and so on around the table. Betting takes place after each new winning hand is exposed. A crude form of Poker in which the skill resides entirely in the betting.

Montana Red Dog Otherwise known as Gutmann. Five cards dealt to each player, one down, one up, then three more one by one with a change at the end. A High Low game with betting between each card. Named after the character played by Sidney Greenstreet in the Maltese Falcon, traditionally the dealer is obliged to provide a card by card commentary on the game, the Aces as they emerge to be referred to as Caspar, Joel, Floyd and Wilmer . . . Greenstreet's first four murder victims.

Bugger Your Neighbour A High Low game in which seven cards are dealt to each player who then selects the best four, passing on the rejects to the player on their left, collecting three from the player on their right. From these, two are rejected and the remaining five placed in a pile and turned one by one. The last card stays down. Bets before the buggery, and between each turn.

Indian The gambler's game. A solitary card is dealt to each player and placed UNSEEN on the forehead. Thus everyone knows your card except you, the point being to use the betting to convince everyone that their card is lower than yours.

Cincinnati High Five cards to each player, plus a flop of five common to all. The latter are turned up one by one, a round of betting in between. Everyone therefore has ten cards from which to choose their best five.

Game One

Mexican Sweat. Seven cards each face down.

EDDIE deals. Each player turns cards until they beat the previous player.

CHRIS: 6H, 6SP, AH, 6D, 5SP, 2H, ACL.

CLIVE: 10CL, KH, 4 SP, 3D, KCL, KD, card unseen.

EDDIE: 9D, 9H, 3SP, QD, 8CL, 7H, AD.

Game Two

is entirely fictional.

Game Three

Montana Red Dog, high, low. with a change. Five cards dealt one by one, first card is down. After fifth card, one change is permitted, down or up. KEVIN deals.

Cards to be arranged in following sequence:

8SP, QD, 6D, KD, 4SP, ASP, JSP, KH, 9D, 8H, JH, 7SP, QH, QSP, 7H, 4H, KSP, 8CL, 3H, 4CL, 5H, 3D, 6CL.

MICKY: Q (hidden), A, 8, Q, 8.

CLIVE: 8(hidden) 4, 9, Q, K.

EDDIE: 6 (hidden) J, J, 7, 3.

KEVIN: K (hidden), K, 7, 4, 4.

MICKY changes ace and gets a five.

EDDIE changes jack and gets a three.

KEVIN changes seven and gets a six.

Game Four

Indian poker. A single card on the forehead, seen only by the other players. CLIVE deals.

CHRIS: 8H.

KEVIN: 3CL.

EDDIE: KCL.

CLIVE: 6SP.

Game Five

Cards irrelevant. CLIVE and KEVIN have the best hands, though CLIVE has the edge.

Game Six.

Cincinnati High. Five cards in the flop common to all. Five cards to each player. Common cards are turned one by one. EDDIE deals.

THE FLOP: K, 10, 7, 10, K (last two remain unseen).

KEVIN: Ace, K, 6, 5, 9.

MICKY: 2, 8, 10, Q, 5.

CLIVE: J, 6, 4, Q, 8.

CHRIS: 7, 7, K, 2, 9.

EDDIE: 3, A, Q, 9, 4.

Sequence of cards: (six hands dealt (including flop), three then two cards): 7, 7, K, 2, 8, 10, A, K, 6, J, 6, 4, 3, A, Q (flop), K, 10, 7, 2, 9, Q, 5,, 5, 9, Q, 8, 9, 4, flop, 10, K.